Myths, Lies, and Denial:

Christian and Secular Counseling In America

by
John Jay Frank

ISBN 978-1-887835-00-8

Published by Minstrel Missions Inc.

II Kings 3:15
or
Ezekiel 33:32

Contact: minstrelmissions@gmail.com
www.minstrelmissions.com

Myths, Lies, and Denial:
Christian and Secular Counseling In America
by John Jay Frank

ISBN 1-887835-00-8
Published by Minstrel Missions Inc.
Contact minstrelmissions@gmail.com

This edition was updated in 2017 with mention of the current dates for some of the resources included.

The main text of the book
is 14 point Arial font (like this line).
The scriptures at the end of each chapter and
the Bibliography are in 12 point Arial font (like this line).

Keywords and book categories:

1. Christian Counseling,
2. Pastoral Care,
3. Church Growth,
4. Bible study,
5. Christian nonfiction.

Contents

Pause and reflect.

Preface

"Ye are the light of the world..." (Matt. 5:14)

When I became a pastor I bought a little black book known as the minister's handbook. It contained several variations of services frequently used such as; baptisms, marriages, and funerals. It provided a bare bones start without which I would have fumbled even more than I did. It omitted such items as the need for a county marriage license signed by two witnesses and the time it takes to heat the water to fill a baptismal tank. Some things are only learned by years of cold, hard, hands on experience.

A search for a similar small book as an introduction to counseling, one of the major areas of pastoring, found only huge volumes. Many of these were very thorough but required much more time than most pastors I know are willing or able to give. After reading many of them (and further study) a pattern began to emerge to the theories and techniques presented. This book is an attempt to distill these down to a handbook size and provide enough background and Biblical references to be useful. Hopefully this will also provide a viewpoint for comparison and perhaps even comfort to those who have wondered if they were all alone. It can be overwhelming to think you are the only one who faces a certain problem.

The perspective in my writing is evangelical. The Bible is the inspired word of God. Our mission is to reach out with His word to all the world. We are to be the light of the world. Counseling should not take precedence over preaching of the word. My hope is that the information in this book will help ease some of that burden.

This is not meant to be a thorough apologetic of Christian counseling or of all the secular theories of psychotherapy. It is not an exhaustive comparison or synthesis of these large and complicated fields. This work is a selective and personal assimilation from my reading and graduate studies in counseling. I hope it is not so terse that it fails to enlighten and reveal helpful insights and not so pontifical that it dismisses unseen potentials which remain.

The main approach is one learned from several years spent as a missionary. I studied the society and culture of the people I lived with as an observant outsider. Upon returning I was able to use that same attitude to describe my own country. I also tried to use insight gained from being a pastor and evangelist in this country. Much time has been spent with pastors and priests from many different churches. We shared our needs and discussed the very troubling situations we all face. Some may label this a negative or one sided description of America but this is a counseling handbook which intends to focus on problems

An impartial look at ourselves may not be flattering but it can be helpful. From time to time over the years I have shared what might be called unwanted human or "natural" wisdom with "hyper-faith" Christians who were facing problems they thought would never effect them (if they only had enough faith). I have also shared spiritual reality with some more down to earth types. If the shoe fits . . ..

I do not take credit for being the originator or the author of any of the theories discussed. I am just a scribe trying to faithfully report what he sees. My contribution is in pulling all these things together, comparing them to scripture, and of course, adding a slant and opinion now and again. I am not trying to prove a point or build or justify any one theory. The goal is to create a brief overview.

Several notes of caution are warranted. First, this work is not neutral. It presents the good and the bad of many systems. However, it is not *pro* or *anti*: science, or religion, or spirituality. Many people would prefer a book which condemns one side and supports another and many such books exist. Next, it is not a series of thrilling stories from a missionary to the land of mental illness. This book is as densely written as a textbook. It can be difficult to read through in one sitting. Finally, the cold statistical presentation of the nature and extent of the problems in our country may be discouraging to read. Count it all joy . . ..

Please bear in mind that there is nothing here that is not also recorded in the Bible in a different form. This comfort from God's word should be kept in mind: "...greater is He that is within you than he that is in the world." (I Jn. 4:4). The evil we face today is not new but the mercies, grace, and comfort we receive to overcome it are new every morning (Lam. 3:22 - 24).

One bias this writer has is that each counseling situation calls for some flexibility or an eclectic approach (Pro. 15:22). The claim cannot be made however that such eclecticism falls within the skills or knowledge of myself or any counselor. Another bias is that God's specific grace, when present, overshadows and supersedes all our natural skills, techniques, and knowledge (II Cor. 10:4). However, just as we cultivate the ground to eat, or build fires for heat, we need the best natural techniques we can find.

The change from preacher to counselor, for this writer, has required great effort to talk less, listen more, keep it simple, and go slow. Another area of growth is learning to treat each person as a unique individual, not as a congregation or one out of many. I can relate the facts in this book to others but I still need to walk the talk, and allow the truth to have full reign in my life (II Sam. 22:36, II Tim. 2:24-25).

Throughout my studies of counseling greater respect has grown for those who, without claiming gifts or wearing labels or earned credentials, do appear to embody, those counseling skills and the personalities which I would most like to emulate. To those individuals who have meant so much to me in my life, be they called mothers and fathers in the faith, or elder friends and mentors, who listen well and counsel wisely, this book is dedicated. All praise, glory, and honor belong to the Lord Jesus Christ. "For unto us a child is born, unto us a son is given...and his name shall be called...Counsellor... (Isaiah 9:6).

(Scripture references for the Preface)

pg. a - Matt. 5:14 - Ye are the light of the world. A city that is set on an hill cannot be hid.

pg. c - Pro. 15:22 - Without counsel purposes are disappointed: but in the multitude of counsellors they are established.

II Cor. 10:4 - (For the weapons of our warfare [are] not carnal, but mighty through God..

.

I Jn. 4:4 - Ye are of God... and have overcome...because greater is he that is in you, than he that is in the world.

Lam. 3:22-24 - [It is of] the LORD'S mercies that we are not consumed, because his compassions fail not. **(23)** [They are] new every morning: great [is] thy faithfulness. **(24)** The LORD [is] my portion, saith my soul; therefore will I hope in him.

pg. d - II Sam. 22:36 - Thou hast also given me the shield of thy salvation: and thy gentleness hath made me great.

II Tim. 2:24-25 - And the servant of the Lord must not strive; but be gentle unto all [men], apt to teach, patient, **(25)** In meekness instructing those that oppose themselves; if God ...will give them repentance to the acknowledging of the truth;

pg. e - Is. 9:6 - For unto us a child is born, unto us a son is given... and his name shall be called Wonderful, Counsellor, The mighty God, The everlasting Father, The Prince of Peace.

Introduction *"...of making many books [there is] no end;" (Ecc. 12:12).*

"What?" "Another book on counseling?" "Who has time to read them all?" That is why this one was written. It is short. It falls somewhere between a long sermon and a short book, barely more than an outline, with about 170 pages of text, 50 pages of scriptures, and a 10 page Bibliography. Its purpose is to be a broad but brief introductory text to help practitioners through the huge volumes or libraries on counseling which they may already own or feel obligated to go out and read. It should help the readers recognize the *source* and *purpose* of the many books, seminars, special programs, video's and other materials that come their way. The goal is to help pastors and counselors self-reflect by asking themselves: **"what do I do when I counsel?"**

Recently a pastor, retiring after thirty-five years of service, related to me his frustration at having worked for years with individuals without seeing any change. The same problems continue to plague certain members of his church today just as much as when he first began. All of his personal involvement, his modeling of a Christian lifestyle and relationships, and his preaching, teaching, and counseling, seemed to have had little or no effect. He felt as though he had failed his flock. **"Can I really be a change agent?"**

Without knowing the cases he was referring to, or his skills, it is reasonable to suggest that just the fact that these people were still coming to church, and were not in even worse shape, may have been a monumental success. We cannot fix everyone. Jesus said "for ye have always the poor with you..." (Matt. 26:11). That may include always having people with us who are emotionally or psychologically destitute and need special care.

The rest of that verse suggests that our priority should be the Lord himself, not just good works. This however, does not relieve us of our responsibility to do our best to help, nor of our expectation for change and growth. We need to have a balance to our expectations and efforts. Does the Gospel promise perfect health, happiness, and complete success to all who believe? Must we read every "fad of the month" counseling book?

Finding a balance is one of several reasons for the title Myths, Lies, and Denial. These three things effect counseling and the controversy that surrounds it. Both the Gospel and psychology attempt to help people. However, they do not have the same goals or standards. The main difference is:

it is not the primary purpose of the Gospel to make bad men into better ones. The purpose is to turn dead men into living men, and to give them the power *to become* sons of God (Jn 1:12).

Unfortunately we do not all become all we were born for. Not everyone uses what they have been given, either in the natural or the spiritual. Neither do we have the means to solve all problems. One of our hardest tasks is to simply live with the knowledge of our limitations. This humility reveals more clearly the grace of our Lord (II Cor. 12:9).

* * * * * * * * *

Three opposing opinions quickly stand out when discussing psychology and counseling as it relates to the Bible and Christians. One school of thought adds certain basic Christian values and scriptural teaching to what is otherwise secular psychology. This tries to create a new "Christian" psychology, psychiatry, or counseling system by presenting a model of man that briefly includes a spiritual dimension. Again note, psychology and the Bible do not have the same standards or goals.

More importantly, psychology is not new. Its work is to collect data and present a systemized view of mankind. Most, if not all, of this was discussed originally in the Bible. This (soft) science merely organizes and confirms what has long been recorded. <u>Myths, Lies, and Denial</u> attempts to show that connection and to point out some of the flaws of science as well as some religious excesses. It is not the purpose of this book to encourage the readers to embrace psychology. The hope is that it will help them sort out some of what is going on.

Another school of thought rejects the science of psychology or counseling outright. They see it as the product of secular humanism that is often opposed to basic Bible truths. It is amusing, but sad, to hear those with this view accept or promote a program, or an analysis of a person's character, or problem, based on Greek philosophy, out-dated or bad psychology, or some other non-Biblical source. This kind of confusion takes place all over. For example, secular therapists have promoted the healing power of forgiveness without revealing the source of that insight.

The third approach, which this book takes, may be called "ecological." This point of view looks at the entire environment: the psychological, biological, cultural, social, religious, and spiritual aspects of man. Counseling must consider more than *either* spiritual *or* psychological. It can affect spirit, soul, and body. The Apostle James is looking at the whole picture when he writes "faith, if it hath not works is dead," (Ja. 2:17).

This is urgently needed because with the break-up of families, communities, and church splits, much of our basic support network, common sense, and wisdom, has been lost or neglected. The Apostle Paul prescribed a type of counseling: "The aged women... may teach the young women..." (Tit. 2:4). Today, divorce has left many older women abandoned, hurting, and in need of care. Others may retire and move south. Where is their teaching to be found?

A pastor too may be the product of a broken home or move frequently. These cases illustrate just two of the many aspects that affect counseling which need to be dealt with. It may be easier to deal only with the Word and power of God but how much power do we really have or use?

A major myth, (imaginary thing), to deal with is the desire for one *easy* book that will help us counsel better. It must include case studies that teach by use of examples rather than by the use of complicated jargon. It should also give step by step directions that will succeed. The Bible can be used that way but it is not easy. This is not an easy book either. There is a demand for answers or great power without effort or cost. This is like the futile search for the fictitious pill or program to help us lose weight without exercising or eating less–that so many people buy.

This book is an introductory overview of some processes and problems in counseling in the United States today. History and religious doctrine are briefly mentioned as well as current psychological theories and Christian approaches to counseling. It presents, as categories and statistics (not in great detail), some of the types of problems counselors face. Over 100 techniques have been included. Some basic guidelines to observe are mentioned, such as tips on referral, and also some of the requirements for becoming a counselor.

It will not make a person into a counselor nor answer specific problems. This is not a "how to" or a "self-help" book. It does provide tips on how to find information concerning specific problems and includes an up-to-date bibliography. Some of the reference works cited are used by professionals in the field, including clergy. To use them effectively usually requires training and practice.

Scripture references have been included for many points and theories. It can be awkward to have to look up a reference so they have been placed at the end of each chapter (Neh. 8:8, Acts 17:11). One of the purposes of this book is to point out the Biblical foundation of counseling. (Matt. 7:24 & 25, I Cor. 1:20, 2:5, 12 & 13).

For anyone struggling to come into the "more abundant life" (Jn. 10:10), this book offers a liberating perspective. It should help pastors and counselors be more confident in their work. For those who wonder when "all things shall be made new" (Rev. 21:5), it can help clear the soil so the seed of the Word of life may be planted, grow, and bear much fruit (Mk. 4:19).

* * * * * * * *

Some major points are highlighted in **bold print** and put in boxes.

A row of asterisks * * * * * * * * has been placed between paragraphs when the topic suddenly changes in the middle of a page.

(Scripture references for the Introduction)

pg. 1 - Ecc. 12:12 - ...of making many books [there is] no end; and much study [is] a weariness of the flesh.

pg. 2 - Matt 26:11 - For ye have the poor always with you; but me ye have not always.

Jn 1:12 - But as many as received him, to them gave he power to become the sons of God, even to them that believe on his name:

pg. 3 - II Cor. 12:9 - ...My grace is sufficient for thee; for my strength is made perfect in weakness. ...

pg. 4 - Ja. 2:17 - Even so faith, if it hath not works, is dead, being alone.

Titus 2:4 - The aged women likewise... that they teach the young women to be sober, (responsible) to love their husbands, to love their children.

pg. 6 - Neh. 8:8 - So they read in the book in the law of God...and gave the sense... to understand the reading.

Acts 17:11 - These were more noble... in that they received the word... and searched the scriptures daily, whether those things were so.

Matt. 7:24-25 - ...whosoever heareth these sayings of mine, and doeth them, I will liken him unto a wise man, which built his house upon a rock; **(25)** And the rain... and the floods came, and the winds blew, ...and it fell not; for it was founded upon a rock.

I Cor. 1:20 - Where [is] the wise? where [is] the scribe? where [is] the disputer of this world? hath not God made foolish the wisdom of this world?

I Cor. 2:5 - That your faith should not stand in the wisdom of men, but in the power of God.

I Cor. 2:12-13 - Now we have received, not the spirit of the world, but the spirit which is of God... the things that are freely given to us of God. **(13)** ...we speak, not in the words which man's wisdom teacheth, but which the Holy Ghost teacheth; comparing spiritual things with spiritual.

Jn 10:10 - ...I am come that they might have life, and that they might have it more abundantly.

Rev. 21:5 - ...Behold, I make all things new.

Mk. 4:19 - And the cares of the world, and the deceitfulness of riches... and lusts... choke the word...

Overview

Section I - introduces three opposing views on counseling, some basic religious doctrine and history, and the problems we face.

Section II - presents three major problems in science, religion, and counseling: myths, lies, and denial.

Section III - explains major theories of personality, and pathology, and compares Christian and secular counseling theorists.

Section IV - presents common techniques used and describes settings and formats.

Section V - gives some guidelines and offers some concluding thoughts.

I - History and Doctrine

> *"I pray not that thou shouldest take them out of the world... They are not of the world..." (Jn. 17:15 & 16).*

Initially, counseling was the work of the wise elder, or holy one, who was thought to speak for God. Moses was in his 80's before he began to be respected for his counsel. Even then he still needed the counsel of his father-in-law. Jethro told him how to avoid burnout from too much work and gave him the criteria for selecting subordinate counselors (Ex. 18:13-26). The Apostle Paul, who gave much advice, was an elder. In one letter he calls himself Paul the aged. His counsel was so valid because he had the Spirit of God (I Cor. 7:40). Their advice covered all areas because the spiritual and the natural were viewed as connected.

That view has often been challenged. The spread of Christianity in Europe began early in the third century with the formation of monasteries. Priests and monks lived separated from the rest of society under a strict system of "règles" (rules), from which came later church systems. In the Latin "religãre" means to bind (by rules or règles). "Religio" (a social bond), is where the word religion comes from. A split in religious orders began in France and spread throughout Europe.

An order of priests arose who were concerned with the welfare of others in society outside the monastery. They considered isolation wrong. They were called priests of the "siècle" (world or age), from which we get our word secular. These priests lived among the "common" people outside the monasteries. Their goal was to help people with the problems of living. They did more than give alms and intercede with prayer. History records the work of those who were the hands, feet, and mouth of the Lord. They worked to help the poor and to change laws to promote justice and to protect the weak from exploitation. It would take many volumes or libraries, including Fox's Book of the Martyrs, to tell their story.

Today the word secular means an exclusive world view. It refers to a complete separation of the church and the state. Science is presented as being in support of a secular world view that defines man's problems and offers solutions to them. It creates theories on: origins, (where we came from or how we got here) evolution, (who we are or are becoming) and the future, (what we are doing and why and how). It does this all the while denying a supernatural spiritual reality or authority. Science, rather than being neutral, is very often coopted by secular humanism to aid in its anti-religion, anti-spiritual, only natural agenda. In modern times the state has absorbed many of the educational and welfare needs of its citizens. The church seems to have lost its role of leadership in dealing with the troubled members of our society.

An uninformed response to the science and culture of the 21th century is a formula for failure. Secular historians have tried to remove religion from its central role in American life by rewriting textbooks and by removing or defacing landmarks. Christianity became more than a Jewish cult by being able to relate and expand to other cultures. It still has a leading role to play in promoting, providing, and defining caregiving and counseling.

Throughout church history there have been splits between a Gospel of Rules (religion), and a Social Gospel (secularism), and a Spiritual Gospel (the supernatural). This third area, the Spiritual, refers to a personal and reciprocal relationship with God in the supernatural sense. Religions that focus on rules of living, and secular systems which focus only on the natural needs of humanity, tend to deny the Divine. To diminish spirituality is to reject one of man's basic attributes. Miracles are by definition rare occurrences but our spiritual desires and relationships are normal. Unfortunately this may get used to isolate or separate us rather than it being a vitalizing force to believers.

Counseling has been broken into these areas too. One view stresses individual responsibility - just obey the rules. Another side accents community involvement - find others who can help. A third view emphasizes spirituality - get help directly from God. These are too often viewed as being in opposition to each other. The Bible offers and encourages all three approaches.

Essential features of Christianity include: a personal relationship with God through Jesus Christ, (the Spiritual), (Jn. 3:5-7, 15:5, I Jn. 1:3). The results of such a relationship would include the desire for and growth toward Holiness, (in one sense the fulfillment of rules), (Ezk. 22:26, Amos 5:15, Ps. 33:3 & 4, Jn. 14:21 & 23, II Cor. 6:17). A further manifestation would be in good works, (the secular), (Is. 58:6 & 7, Matt. 25:35-37 & 40, Eph. 2:10, Ja. 1:27, 2:18). These are inseparable components of the Christian faith. The study of the Bible (Ps. 119:105, I Cor. 10:11), and fellowship with other Christians (Pro. 27:17, Heb. 10:25), and others around us are all important elements.

Historically, these aspects of Christianity have battled for preeminence. The perfect balance is not likely to emerge but we can be aware of the swings in emphasis and style. The style and government of churches are also areas of divisiveness. Some churches emphasize a more sacramental format. Others follow the style that arose from the Oxford revivals and employ a university lecture model. Another style includes greater emphasis on music and worship. Variations in rules for membership, voting, and leadership exist. Different blends of these exist. These are not essential features of doctrine no matter how many people fight and die over them!

Contrary to myth, few if any essential or basic doctrines and interpretations of scripture are in dispute among Christian churches. Application does vary. This may seem like an outrageous thing to say. One merely has to point to the differences over sacraments, or the hatred and strife that exists between Protestants and Catholics in Ireland, the racism in the Reformed church in South Africa, or the wars in Bosnia, Armenia, or elsewhere, to find grievous religious disputes.

The divisions in our own country among churches of even closer persuasion and proximity may run a gauntlet through high/low, modern/traditional, liberal/conservative, spectrums over nonessentials some would still call damnable heresy or cardinal sin. However, we Christians do not have doctrinal disputes over essential features of our faith. We hang convenient religious labels on some things we do to justify them and our uniqueness. Whether it is for racial, political, or financial reasons, we can act very much like the church in Corinth that Paul severely rebuked (I Cor. 1:13, 3:3, 12:20, Eph. 4:4).

In countries where Buddhist, Hindu, or Islamic beliefs prevail many people see "Christian" America as not only divided but also immoral, violent, and greedy. This in part is due to our TV programs and movies and the openness with which our news media report on the worst aspects of our lifestyle. Our custom of putting the infirm and the elderly into nursing homes instead of caring for them at home, and the obvious division between white and black churches here, is looked upon as evil. The problems and divisions that exist are not at the level of doctrine as much as they are really the result of personal preference or of faulty practice. **A lack of love is a violation of Christian doctrine. It is not a variation or different belief system found in scripture**. We aim high but often miss.

These problems have helped to fuel the rise of a humanist world view. The attempt is often made to discredit the Bible by pointing to the Crusades, or the Inquisition, or the persecution of Galileo, or a Victorian hypocrisy, or immorality within the clergy, and even the belief that the earth is flat and the center of the universe! This presupposes a successful grand theocracy. Such a state has never existed, not in the book of Acts, nor in Rome. Even Adolph Hitler was pictured in shining armor, riding on a white horse, with a caption proclaiming he was the Messiah who had returned to establish his thousand-year reign.

Religion is often corrupted for political ends, even wars. A God fearing, Bible believing government can be an immense force for good. However, the evil men do in the name of religion tarnishes only them, not God. Today, heros of the faith, like those recorded in the eleventh chapter of Hebrews, continue "...to look for a city whose builder and maker [is] God."

Chapter I Review

We are not of the world but in it. Spiritual elders may be counselors. The Spiritual has been tied to, and separated from, the natural. Religion, either as a system of rules, or as Spiritual reality, has been separated from the secular. This split exists in Christianity and counseling. All three areas are needed. Little conflict exists over essential doctrines but practices do differ. Religion and science can get misused for personal and political purposes.

(Scripture references for chapter I)

pg. 9

John 17:15 & 16 - I pray not that thou shouldest take them out of the world, but that thou shouldest keep them from the evil. **(16)** They are not of the world, even as I am not of the world.

Ex 18:13-26 - **(13)** And it came to pass on the morrow, that Moses sat to judge the people: and the people stood by Moses from the morning unto the evening. **(14)** And when Moses' father in law saw all that he did to the people, he said, What [is] this thing that thou doest to the people? why sittest thou thyself alone, and all the people stand by thee from morning unto even? **(15)** And Moses said unto his father in law, Because the people come unto me to enquire of God: **(16)** When they have a matter, they come unto me; and I judge between one and another, and I do make [them] know the statutes of God, and his laws. (17) And Moses' father in law said unto him, The thing that thou doest [is] not good. **(18)** Thou wilt surely wear away, both thou, and this people that [is] with thee: for this thing [is] too heavy for thee; thou art not able to perform it thyself alone. **(19)** Hearken now unto my voice, I will give thee counsel, and God shall be with thee: Be thou for the people to God-ward, that thou mayest bring the causes unto God: **(20)** And thou shalt teach them ordinances and laws, and shalt shew them the way wherein they must walk, and the work that they must do. **(21)** Moreover thou shalt provide out of all the people able men such as fear God, men of truth, hating covetousness; and place [such] over them, [to be] rulers of thousands, [and] rulers of hundreds, rulers of fifties, and rulers of tens: **(22)** And let them judge the people at all seasons: and it shall be, [that] every great matter they shall bring unto thee, but every small matter they shall judge: so shall it be easier for thyself, and they shall bear [the burden] with thee. **(23)** If thou shalt do this thing, and God command thee [so], then thou shalt be able to endure, and all this people shall also go to their place in peace. **(24)** So Moses hearkened to the voice of his father in law, and did all that he had said. **(25)** And Moses chose able men out of all Israel, and made them heads over the people, rulers of thousands, rulers of hundreds, rulers of fifties, and rulers of tens. **(26)** And they judged the people at all seasons: the hard causes they brought unto Moses, but every small matter they judged themselves.

I Cor. 7:40 - ...I think also that I have the Spirit of God.

pg. 12

Jn. 3:5-7 - Jesus answered... Except a man be born of water and [of] the Spirit, he cannot enter into the kingdom of God. **(6)** That which is born of the flesh is flesh; and that which is born of the Spirit is spirit. **(7)** Marvel not that I said unto thee, Ye must be born again.

Jn. 15:5 - I am the vine, ye [are] the branches: He that abideth in me, and I in him, the same bringeth forth much fruit: for without me ye can do nothing.

I Jn. 1:3 - ...and truly our fellowship [is] with the Father, and with his Son Jesus Christ.

Ezek. 22:26 - Her priests have violated my law and have profaned mine holy things: they have put no difference between the holy and profane, neither have they shewed [difference] between the unclean and the clean,...

Amos 5:15 - Hate the evil, and love the good, and establish judgment in the gate:...

Ps. 33:3-4 - For the word of the Lord [is] right; and all his works are [done] in truth. **(4)** He loveth righteousness and judgement:...

Jn. 14:21 & 23 - He that hath my commandments, and keepeth them, he it is that loveth me: and he that loveth me shall be loved of my Father, and I will love him, and will manifest myself to him. **(23)** Jesus answered and said unto him, If a man love me, he will keep my words: and my Father will love him, and we will come unto him, and make our abode with him.

II Cor. 6:17 - Wherefore come out from among them, and be ye separate, saith the Lord, and touch not the unclean [thing]; and I will receive you,

Is. 58:6-7 - [Is] not this the fast that I have chosen? to loose the bands of wickedness, to undo the heavy burdens, and to let the oppressed go free, and that ye break every yoke? **(7)** [Is it] not to deal thy bread to the hungry, and that thou bring the poor that are cast out to thy house? when thou seest the naked, that thou cover him;...

Matt. 25:35-37, & 40 - For I was an hungred, and ye gave me meat: ... thirsty, and ye gave me drink: ...a stranger, and ye took me in: **(36)** Naked, and ye clothed me: ...sick, and ye visited me: ...in prison, and ye came unto me. **(37)** Then shall the righteous answer him, saying, Lord, when...? **(40)** And the King shall answer and say unto them, Verily I say unto you, Inasmuch as ye have done [it] unto one of the least of these my brethren, ye have done [it] unto me.

Eph. 2:10 - For we are his workmanship, created in Christ Jesus unto good works, which God hath before ordained that we should walk in them.

Ja. 1:27 & 2:18 - Pure religion and undefiled before God and the Father is this, To visit the fatherless and widows in their affliction, [and] to keep himself unspotted from the world. **(18)** Yea, a man may say, Thou hast faith, and I have works: shew me thy faith without thy works, and I will shew thee my faith by my works.

Ps. 119:105 - Thy word [is] a lamp unto my feet, and a light unto my path.

I Cor. 10:11 - Now all these things happened unto them for ensamples: and they are written for our admonition, upon whom the ends of the world are come.

Pro. 27:17 - Iron sharpeneth iron; so a man sharpeneth the countenance of his friend.

Heb. 10:25 - Not forsaking the assembling of ourselves together, as the manner of some [is]; but exhorting [one another]: ...the more, as ye see the day approaching.

pg. 13
I Cor. 1:13, 3:3, 12:20 - Is Christ divided?... **(3)** For ye are yet carnal ...there is among you envying, and strife, and divisions... (20) now [are they] many members, but one body.

Eph. 4:4 - [There is] one body...

pg. 14
Heb. 11:10 & 16 - For he looked for a city which hath foundations, whose builder and maker [is] God. **(16)** - But now they desire a better [country], that is, an heavenly: wherefore God is not ashamed to be called their God: for he hath prepared for them a city.

II - Life in the U.S.A.

"...a man of sorrows, and acquainted with grief..." (Isaiah 53:3).

What sorts of problems and situations are counselors likely to face? The United States has more people in church and in prison than any other country in the world. The crack cocaine epidemic is just a small part of the reason. There are 43 million people here, or about 15% of the population, with chronic disabilities. Many receive some kind of financial help such as Social Security Disability Insurance. In 1991 Worker Compensation paid out $70 billion due to accidents occurring on the job, many that could have easily been prevented. About 40% of the jobs here are part-time with no benefits. The U.S. has over 10 million full-time workers who fall below the poverty level. Millions of involuntarily jobless and homeless.

Over half of our marriages end in divorce, 60% of our children live with only one parent and 25% live in poverty. Less than 5% of our families live the traditional model of a working husband with a wife who stays home to take care of the children. Latch key kids are the norm not the exception. Each year there are 3 million children found to be abused and/or neglected out of twice that many complaints filed. This includes over 2,000 cases of a parent killing his or her own child. Another 1.5 million get killed by abortion yearly.

Suicide was the second leading cause of deaths among teenagers after auto "accidents." Recently murder has taken first place, so suicide is third place. Unwed teen pregnancies are at an epidemic level (26% of all births). So are eating disorders such as anorexia and bulimia. Some of our children are starving to death as though they were in a famine.

As Many as 60% of those who have eating disorders may have been the victims of rape or incest (Lev. 18:6, Ezek. 22:11). It is estimated that between one in three and one in four women in this country were molested as children and one in ten to one in seven men were victims of sexual abuse when they were children. Of over 100,000 rapes reported here last year less than one fifth of the perpetrators were convicted and punished.

Our homicide rate plus the number of vehicular deaths due to drunk driving is as high as the death toll from the civil wars and famines of many countries. Our capital city vies for the title of "the murder capital of the world." America has over 10,000 handgun murders a year. New York City has had to set aside an entire school for children who are the survivors of violent crime or who have had someone in their immediate family murdered. Their grief process can be so intense that these children need to be separated from other children and adults who do not understand the emotional turmoil they are experiencing. Pastors can hardly understand all this.

The United States ranks very poorly, thirtieth in the world, on infant mortality – not counting abortion. We have more infants dying at birth, or shortly thereafter, than many third world nations. At the other end of life, "granny dumping" refers to the practice here of abandoning an estimated 200,000 elderly people by the front doors of hospitals each year.

The AIDS epidemic is spreading in our inner cities as fast as it is in the poorest African nations. There are an estimated 40 million alcoholics in America and 28 million children of alcoholics who have grown up in, or are now being raised in, dysfunctional alcoholic families. A good question to ask is: "why does one person from a damaging environment need counseling and another person gets elected President, or Speaker of the House?"

If we tried to limit these tragedies we might have less need for counselors. Just over half the children here in America receive inoculations for preventable, childhood diseases. China does more than we do, in this area of protecting children from disease, - and they practice infanticide.

The Civil Rights act of 1964 makes it illegal to discriminate against a person due to their race, culture, or nation of origin. It has expanded to include: sex, religion, age, and recently disability (Lev. 19:14 & 32, Jer. 22:13, Mal. 3:5, Gal. 3:28, Ja. 5:4). Lawsuits are needed to enforce it.

Most religious organizations are not subject to the Americans with Disabilities Act of 1990 (except for employment, Title I). There are churches that keep out the lame and the blind by their architecture or by how they use technology. Charlatans can act as healing "prophets" because most people do not know health statistics such as: 80% of the men in America will suffer from back pain (I Pet. 4:17).

We are rightly called a nation in deep denial. Complaints abound over the billions of dollars worth of drugs smuggled into our country. At the same time we force other nations to buy billions of dollars worth of our addicting, death causing, tobacco. We are also the number one arms dealer in the world (Gal. 6:7).

We plunder the resources of other nations to feed our pets. Our own land, water, air, and food are now just as polluted as theirs. We are greedy, violent, and selfish. With just 6% of the world's population here we consume 60% of its resources. Over half the people of the world live on less than $400 per person, per year. We like to think we are the best nation in the world. We may very well be, but the words of the song are true too: "It's me, it's me, it's me, Oh Lord, standing in the need of prayer." Billy Graham prayed for repentance for this nation during the inauguration of the President in January 1993 (II Chron. 7:14, I Cor. 11:31). We pray for a God fearing government, but we may instead get what we deserve. We may all be able to agree on this. It is harder to agree on why these things happen or what can be done about them.

People seek counseling, voluntarily or not, for an enormous variety of reasons. These may be labeled: medical, psychological (mental or emotional,) societal, behavioral, addictive, religious or spiritual problems. They may result from the trauma (past or present) of: accidents or injury, crimes, wars. natural disasters, or even pollution. Help is sought by families dealing with congenital problems (birth defects). Violence in the family; the physical, verbal, or sexual abuse of children, spouses, the elderly, or their neglect, is rampant. Counseling may be needed by a family member or caregiver close to someone with a severe problem (burnout), or who causes it (guilt).

Lists of other problems include: divorce, difficulty with relationships, substance abuse, rape, eating disorders (obesity, anorexia, or bulimia), sexual dysfunction or inappropriate or absent behaviors, failures, fears, stress, anxiety, difficulty with school or employment, poverty, prejudice or discrimination, loneliness, loss of ability, chronic pain, illness, death, loss of values or status, suicide ideation, depression, nightmares, being out of touch with reality, or having imaginary problems.

It helps to have an idea of what problems exist, though their definitions change. **The problem a client presents may not be the only one they have** (Job 10:1, Ps. 109:22). After a counselor has gained the trust of a person other things emerge. The problem itself may direct the style and source of intervention.

For further details of problems consult: The Merck Manual of Diagnosis and Therapy, (ed. R. Berkow, 19th edition, 2011). This is used in the medical profession. Having a medical dictionary with it, such as Tabers's Cyclopedic Medical Dictionary helps. Psychological problems are dealt with in The Comprehensive Textbook of Psychiatry, by Kaplan & Sadock, (1989). The primary source to use is The Diagnostic and Statistical Manual of Mental Disorders, [now the DSM-V,], (American Psychiatric Assoc., 2013), Another related reference, which uses case studies, is the DSM-IV Casebook (Spitzer et. al., 1994).

The DSM-V is so complete and detailed it is used as an international standard. The Casebook includes cases from other countries to help avoid cultural and religious bias. For instance, according to the DSM IV, hearing the voice of a spirit, or seeing a spirit, or giving credit to a spirit for being the cause of some problem, is not a psychological problem if contact with the "spirit world" is a commonly accepted part of a person's culture.

This does not only apply to "primitive" third world countries. It would include certain groups in the United States. When the results of such spirit contact create problems, such as: dramatic and harmful changes in a person's lifestyle, getting hurt, violent actions, or wandering and getting lost, those problems are what need to be treated. The person should not be labeled schizophrenic or psychotic because of their beliefs.

A glaring difference to note between Christian and secular counseling books is that Christian writers usually "sanitize" or clean up their work. Secular case studies retain the foul language, and give descriptions of vile behaviors, exhibited in certain cases (Eph. 5:12). Mental illness is not the only place where obscenity is common. Bitter marriage conflicts, even some that respond well to counseling, can be very ugly to read about, let alone deal with in person. Working with troubled children can be quite shocking.

A less graphic source of helpful information that is long but easy to read is the encyclopedic work: Resources for Christian Counseling Series, edited by Gary Collins. It has many different contributors and is published by Word, in Texas. By 1995 there were about thirty volumes and more are planned. Each one focuses on one problem area such as: Counseling the Adult Child of an Alcoholic, Depression, or Eating Disorders. Each volume is usually between two and three hundred pages in length, and costs under $15.

CHAPTER II REVIEW

What problems and conditions have you dealt with? Include bereavement counseling. What source materials do you use? Can you find other sources?

(Scripture References for chapter II)

pg. 19

Is. 53:3 - He is despised and rejected of men; a man of sorrows, and acquainted with grief: and we hid as it were [our] faces from him; he was despised, and we esteemed him not.

pg. 20 - Lev. 18:6 - None of you shall approach to any that is near of kin to him to uncover [their] nakedness...

Ezek. 22:11 - ...and another hath lewdly defiled his daughter in law; and another in thee hath humbled his sister, his father's daughter.

pg. 21 - Lev. 19:14 & 32 - Thou shalt not curse the deaf, nor put a stumbling block before the blind... **(32)** honour the face of the old man...

Jer. 22:13 - Woe unto him that... useth his neighbour's service without wages, and giveth him not for his work;

Mal. 3:5 - ...I will be a swift witness against... those that oppress the hireling in [his] wages...

Gal. 3:28 - There is neither Jew nor Greek... bond nor free... male nor female: for ye are all one in Christ...

Ja. 5:4 - Behold, the hire of the labourers... which is of you kept back by fraud, crieth...

pg. 22 - I Pet. 4:17 - ...judgment must begin at the house of God...

Gal. 6:7 - Be not deceived; God is not mocked: for whatsoever a man soweth, that shall he also reap.

II Chron. 7:14 - If my people, which are called by my name, shall humble themselves, and pray, and seek my face, and turn from their wicked ways; then will I hear from heaven, and will forgive their sin, and will heal their land.

I Cor. 11:31 - For if we would judge ourselves, we should not be judged.

pg. 23 - Job 10:1 - My soul is weary of my life; I will leave my complaint upon myself; I will speak in the bitterness of my soul.

Ps. 109:22 - For I [am] poor and needy, and my heart is wounded within me.

pg. 25 - Eph. 5:12 - For it is a shame to even speak of those things which are done of them in secret.

III - Secular Myths

"...avoiding... opposition of science falsely so-called:" (I Tim. 6:20).

Before anyone can begin to deal with a problem they must be aware that they have one. Conviction and guilt, failure and crisis, or trusting someone else's opinion when they point out a problem are the usual ways people come to recognize they have a problem. A person may be so hard-hearted, defensive, or unable to trust, that he or she will ignore or refuse these signs and warnings. Living with myths, lies, and denial can increase that resistance and obstruct change. This happens with individuals, groups, or countries.

A myth is a: person, thing, idea, goal, or image, assumed to be reality, which ignores the facts. Belief in a myth is not a problem. It is one ingredient of hope and stability. The pervasiveness and kinds of myths in our lives, and how we accommodate them, can be a problem. We have been called a nation in denial (Deut. 32:28). Our mass media, advertising, and politics highlight this. Our national myths reveal it too. A "we can do anything" mentality, "positivism," "optimism," and plain old fashioned pride are attitudes that define us to ourselves and to visiting foreigners or others viewing us from abroad as well.

Greed, and myths of wealth, have produced a boom in gambling by State Lottery. People will still play a lottery (a voluntary taxation) even with only a one in sixty million chance at winning. Some of our state governments are being financed by games of chance. Our national budget is a myth written so as to hide our debt. We have churches financed by Bingo gambling. Credit card use enslaves those who deny they cannot afford things. Those who are overcome by a compulsive need to buy, or to take risks, turn to groups like Debtors or Gamblers Anonymous.

Our national media portrays cowboys and gangsters as heros while ignoring the sorrow and evil of those characters. Hollywood exports these myths around the world. We think of ourselves as people who came from and are "pioneers" and "rugged individuals" living in "the land of equal opportunity." Only a minority make their living as self-employed entrepreneurs. Businesses may rely on government subsidies, then complain about taxes and welfare.

We love the notion of "romantic love" and the controlling power of emotion which are both contrary to a Biblical concept of love (I Cor. 13). We have the highest marriage rate in the world, and the highest divorce rate. The divorce rate is even higher after our great number of second marriages, but the romantic myth of love prevails for many over the Biblical notion of sacrifice, commitment, and responsibility.

We believe universal education will provide everyone with the tools to be successful but we have an illiteracy rate higher than many poorer countries. Our myth of equal opportunity ignores the fact that, in many states, rich school districts spend ten times more per student than do poorer districts. Instead of spending enough to teach people to read we lower standards and inflate grades. Universal education simply cannot work if we do not practice it.

It cannot work with God and the Bible excluded (I Cor. 8:1). The Bible is still the #1 best-seller in the country yet religious books are excluded from mention on "best seller" lists. The non-establishment clause of our constitution has been twisted to mean the exclusion of all religion instead of simply meaning that we do not have a state mandated religion. The history taught in our schools is used to instill the secular myth of a non-religious America. Even though it is not illegal to mention God, religion, or the Bible in public schools, the lie of the separation of church and state has been foisted on the public schools by the fear of the expense of just having to defend against lawsuits.

Liberal voices are now joining the outcry against the exclusion of information on religious life in America in the public schools. What that has produced however is the freedom to introduce: cults, new age, eastern religions, native American religions, and "the basic psychological need" of humans for religion (II Cor. 2:11, Col. 2:8). With whatever space and time is left mention may be made, in social studies textbooks and classes, of our Judeo-Christian heritage. In reality, where this "balanced" approach is being used, very little time is left for the expression of any Christian beliefs.

* * * * * * * * *

One of our most cherished myths is science. Scientific theories must be as complete, simple, and precise as possible (this is called parsimony). They should stimulate thought as to ways they can be disproved, not just verified and validated. Theories need to be tested by scientific technique which is the process of systematic observation, investigation, and experimentation. The purpose is to label, and to be able to explain, control, and predict. One of the chief assumptions of science is that there is a cause for every effect and that every effect will cause some other effect. The job of the scientist is simply to find these and express them. Then technicians use them.

This assumption is useful in that it permits unrestricted research, but it is also a denial of the absolutes of a creator (without a cause), and our free choice. Referring to a Big Bang instead of to God is denial, not theory. In psychology, the fact of a person's free choice may be undermined by the assumption that our choices were produced by an endless string of causes. Finding some of those causes may help bring change or healing. This should allow freedom to make responsible choices not excuses.

Looking at some specific "scientific" lies reveals the depth of our cultural denial. All of the attempts to discover a "missing link" to prove the theory of evolution have resulted in failure and often outright fraud. The government pays for much of this research. Fake pictures and theories continue to be published in textbooks used in public schools without a disclaimer given. The scientific mystique of radioactive carbon 14 dating suggests an authoritative knowledge of how old things are. However, the rate of decay is measured against old, unproven theories, and an unprovable assumption of consistency in the rate of decay. Creationism is labeled "unscientific" and excluded for fear of establishing a state religion. The unprovable theories of Secular Humanism have become the state supported religion. Creationists are labeled as defending the Bible instead of as scientists questioning the false claims of secular science.

Several of our scientific heros may have distorted the truth for their own ends. Sigmund Freud heard many of his patients recount incidents of being molested as children. Rather than upset his rich male patrons in high society (and thus reduce his income), he came up with theories of sexual drives and development. He refused to face the problem of incest that actually existed. His theories are a pseudo-scientific way of saying what a pedophile or child molester claims after being arrested and put on trial, namely; "the little girl or boy wanted to have, or imagined having, sex."

Another icon of American science the venerated Dr. Margaret Mead, is considered by many to be a dean of American Cultural Anthropology. Her book Coming of Age In Samoa, (1928), describes her experiences among a South Pacific island people who, according to her observations, were uninhibited by old fashioned Bible morality. They were free to engage in sexual exploration without heeding "backward" western taboos on marriage. This was a cornerstone work on ethical relativity among different cultures. This theory is used to subvert the presentation of standards of decency. Whenever the attempt to apply Biblical standards is made they may get rejected for being "culturally biased" based on "scientific" studies of this nature.

Years later, after much damage had been done, the island was revisited. The old men there still remembered the young white woman who came to them seeking unbridled sexual experiences which they obliged, since she was not one of their own people, and was obviously a savage who had no moral standards. That young American graduate student on a fantasy island sexual holiday became famous for practicing, and for helping to develop, the method that is technically called scientific participant observation (in this case it is also know as fornication or promiscuity). Her work is touted as an example of the pioneering use of scientific technique in the social sciences. The term “sin” is not considered scientific.

Dr. Alfred Kinsey is another social scientist lauded for his pioneering work. He supposedly demonstrated, in the 1940's and 50's, that human sexuality could be researched *objectively.* His work "corrected" popular misconceptions. He found that homosexuality occurs in 10% of the population. However, he padded his statistical surveys by using prison populations which had a high number of people who engaged in homosexual acts.

He was warned that this was improper methodology and would distort his results. Other researchers place the number at less than 1%. Kinsey's work has been used to justify removing homosexuality as a disorder in the Diagnostic and Statistical Manual of Mental Disorders. Now some schools use textbooks that present homosexuality as a normal human variant. Those same schools exclude the Bible, God, and the Ten Commandments. This call for diversity includes demands for laws to grant special treatment to this group.

Those who have a perverse personal agenda will make, believe, and spread lies (Lev. 18:22, 20:13, Jn. 8:44, Ro. 1:27, Rev. 22:15). This is not unbiased science. A less well known finding made by Dr. Kinsey was that pedophilia is also a common sexual tendency in America which he concluded was not harmful to children. Can we next expect a massive social movement to grant special rights and exposure to child molesters?

That fraudulent research also supported the lie of a genetic homosexual predisposition. This is more than an anti-discrimination fight. It is propagation of a lifestyle choice. Over 46,000 women die of breast cancer each year. However, research on AIDS, which is killing 4,000 people yearly, receives greater funding, ten times as much, than research on breast cancer, due to the political activism of gay rights groups.

The battle over abortion is another example of the use of "scientific" lies and distortion. The definition of life was thrown out by the U.S. Supreme Court because a few "scientists" refuted it. The need to spare the victims of rape and incest was used to justify de-humanizing and killing the unborn. Working at preventing rape and incest was not considered. Instead, re-traumatizing the victim with an abortion rather than serious prosecution of the criminal was the only solution to the problem offered.

What actually takes place is that more than fifty times as many abortions are performed as belated birth control rather than for the purpose of helping rape victims. In fact the number of rapes, and what are now called "date rapes," may have increased because it is "easy" to take care of almost any by-product of sexual behavior. Abstinence is dismissed as unrealistic. Instead, "safe sex" using condoms is taught. The claim of 99% protection from disease and pregnancy is false. Note the caveat, “if used correctly.” They are more like 33% fallible.

The evil specter of women being mutilated or killed by "unsafe" back alley abortions was further useful ammunition in the fight to get "safe" abortions. The fact is ignored that due to the enormous number of these still very dangerous surgical procedures performed each year there are now more women hurt by legal abortions than were ever hurt by the illegal kind. The right of "choice" being demanded is really the right to choose to engage in a behavior (sex) without bearing the consequences. This is a legal right no one has in most spheres of behavior.

* * * * * * * * *

One final misuse or myth of science to consider is the claim that "faith" or God cannot be proven or dealt with scientifically. This distortion is heralded by those who claim God does not exist. It is based on an ignorance of the theory of science and the misuse of scientific tools and criteria. The truth is that nothing is proven by science. Science only gives answers as probabilities, within certain stated conditions, using specified techniques, within specific parameters.

Well developed *scientific* techniques and tools appropriate for examining issues of faith do exist. Obviously it would be hard to try to find the temperature of a glass of warm water using a scale that measured pounds and ounces. A thermometer calibrated between 32 and 212 degrees Fahrenheit could not measure the heat of a nuclear explosion. A shovel is the wrong instrument for astronomers to look at stars through, and a telescope is not usually used by a geologist mining in a cave. How information is reported also differs for different activities. A home run does not give a team six points and a soccer goal does not earn two points. Scientific evidence of the existence of God will not automatically make a believer out of a skeptic, nor allow the scientist to manipulate or control God. Faith and God are as "provable" as any research topics of this nature - when appropriate scientific standards, questions, techniques, measurements and goals are used.

* * * * * * * *

The question raised by pointing out these myths and lies is; when we face a client, even a Christian client, "what do they really believe?" "Coming of Age in America" means being taught "scientific" concepts that are contrary to the Bible and learning that truth is relative and can be, and often is, manipulated (Is. 66:4, Ps. 33:10 & 11, II Tim 4:3 & 4). Christians and non-Christians seem to have separate compartments in their thinking. Religion and the Bible fit in one sphere, while science (supported by miracles of technology) fits in another. The science we believe in may be more mythical than our religion! However, we appear to have a "genetic disposition" for truth (sometimes called a conscience). It takes a lot of emotional energy and support from others to constantly believe a lie and to deny the truth. Counsel, and life change, may be resisted until myths, lies, and denial are exposed and dealt with.

Chapter III Review

These scientific philosophies are not just the stuff of lofty academia or high-brow debate. When children try to negotiate a rule on the basis that so-and-so's parents let him or her do it, they are employing ethical relativity. Often questions about the authority of: a rule, or of God's word, or of a standard interpretation of the Bible, may be based on some misapplication of science or the belief that all religion is man-made.

Myths have been around a long time. When Jesus told the Pharisees the truth would make them free their response was that as Abraham's seed they had never been slaves (Jn. 8:32 & 33). They claimed this despite the fact of their bondage under Roman occupation and their history of captivity in Assyria and Babylon. That is an example of denial. Jesus then refers to them as children of the devil, who is the father of all lies: big or little ones, black or white ones.

Myths may be less blatant untruths. We have a pervasive cultural myth about youth and immortality. This seems to go along with our commercial economy and breed a greater disrespect for the elderly. Another popular myth is that physical beauty equals worth. This contributes to discrimination against less than perfect people in several ways. The TV and movie actors in other countries often look like ordinary people. They are not all young, skinny, and "beautiful."

This chapter, and the next two, explores myths, lies, and denial. For some this is fun, for others it is shameful to even mention these things. It is hoped that this will give some idea of the background conditions under which counseling takes place. **The point is not that exposing or revealing untruths is the work of counseling.** Knowing when, or even if, to expose or confront is essential. It is not the job of a counselor to brutalize a client in the name of the truth. This point will be considered again in the chapter on Guidelines. What other myths, or the making of other myths, do you see in yourself and in counseling? One is the myth that counseling can solve any problem! Another myth is that we can preach the Gospel without regard to or knowledge of the cultural context.

(Scripture References for Chapter III)

pg. 27- I Tim. 6:20 - O Timothy, keep that which is committed to thy trust, avoiding profane [and] vain babblings, and oppositions of science falsely so called.

Deut. 32:28 - For they [are] a nation void of counsel...

pg. 28 - I Cor. 13 - Though I speak with the tongues of men and of
angels, and have not charity, I am become [as] sounding brass, or
a tinkling cymbal. **(2)** And though I have [the gift of] prophecy, and
understand all mysteries, and all knowledge; and though I have all
faith, so that I could remove mountains, and have not charity, I am
nothing. **(3)** And though I bestow all my goods to feed [the poor],
and though I give my body to be burned, and have not charity, it
profiteth me nothing. **(4)** Charity suffereth long, [and] is kind; charity
envieth not; charity vaunteth not itself, is not puffed up, **(5)** Doth not
behave itself unseemly, seeketh not her own, is not easily
provoked, thinketh no evil; **(6)** Rejoiceth not in iniquity, but rejoiceth

in the truth; **(7)** Beareth all things, believeth all things, hopeth all things, endureth all things. **(8)** Charity never faileth: but whether [there be] prophecies, they shall fail; whether [there be] tongues, they shall cease; whether [there be] knowledge, it shall vanish away. **(9)** For we know in part, and we prophesy in part. **(10)** But when that which is perfect is come, then that which is in part shall be done away. **(11)** When I was a child, I spake as a child, I understood as a child, I thought as a child: but when I became a man, I put away childish things. **(12)** For now we see through a glass, darkly; but then face to face: now I know in part; but then shall I know even as also I am known. **(13)** And now abideth faith, hope, charity, these three; but the greatest of these [is] charity.

pg. 29
I Cor. 8:1 - ...knowledge puffeth up, but charity edifieth.

pg.30
II Cor. 2:11 - Lest Satan should get an advantage of us: for we are not ignorant of his devices.

Col. 2:8 - Beware lest any man spoil you through philosophy and vain deceit, after the tradition of men, ...and not after Christ.

pg. 33
Lev. 18:22, 20:13 - Thou shalt not lie with mankind, as with womankind: it [is] abomination. **(13)** If a man also lie with mankind, as he lieth with a woman, both of them have committed an abomination: they shall surely be put to death; their blood [shall be] upon them.

Jn. 8:44 - Ye are of [your] father the devil, and the lusts of your father ye will do. He was a murderer from the beginning, and abode not in the truth, because there is no truth in him. When he speaketh a lie, he speaketh of his own: for he is a liar, and the father of it.

Ro. 1:27 - And likewise also the men, leaving the natural use of the woman, burned in their lust one toward another; men with men working that which is unseemly, and receiving in themselves that recompense of their error.

Rev. 22:15 - For without [are] dogs, and sorcerers, and whoremongers, and murderers, and idolaters, and whosoever loveth and maketh a lie.

pg. 36
Is. 66:4 - I also will choose their delusions, and will bring their fears upon them; because when I called, none did answer; when I spake, they did not hear: but they did evil before mine eyes, and chose [that] in which I delighted not.

Ps. 33:10 & 11 - The Lord bringeth the counsel of the heathen to nought: he maketh the devices of the people of none effect. **(11)** The counsel of the Lord standeth for ever, the thoughts of his heart to all generations.

II Tim. 4:3-4 - For... they will not endure sound doctrine; but after their own lusts shall they heap to themselves teachers, having itching ears; **(4)** And they shall turn ... from the truth, and ...be turned unto fables.

Pg. 37
Jn. 8:32 & 33 - And ye shall know the truth, and the truth shall make you free. **(33)** They answered him, We be Abraham's seed, and were never in bondage to any man, how sayest thou: Ye shall be made free?

IV - Religious Myths,

*"And ye shall know the truth,
and the truth shall make you free."
(Jn. 8:32).*

Scientific technique has been utilized on just about everything, from music to dreams. The term "scientific" adds authority to what might otherwise be labeled opinion or disbelief. There are at least three ways it has been misapplied to the content of religion: 1) Higher Criticism, 2) the study of myths and legends by Carl Jung and Joseph Campbell, and 3) the misapplication of Systematic Theology.

The expression *critical analysis* of the Bible implies the use of the latest scientific techniques. This includes the use of the most advanced and sophisticated technology. The value of a systematic approach is that it allows other researchers to repeat a study to confirm or disprove the findings. This can be a useful tool. Not all critical analysis is fraudulent.

Textual criticism, called lower criticism, focuses on the material of the text. Its purpose is to restore the original wording. Restoration may be of a mere fragment with only a single letter. It may be done on a full scroll or a small section that has been obscured by age, or damaged by fire, water, or other misuse, or simply miscopied. New findings of texts of the Bible or of other ancient writings can shed light on the Bible.

Form Criticism is the practice of describing a portion of scripture as a narrative (talking about God), or as a discourse (God talking). The Psalms have been classified by form as: Psalms of thanksgiving, laments, royal Psalms, or liturgical Psalms. The form or order of presenting the miracles of Jesus in the New Testament has been noted. In the Gospel of Luke every other miracle concerns a gentile, perhaps to highlight the fact that the ministry of Christ went beyond the Jews and His purposes were worldwide. The seven miracles prsented in the Gospel of John are placed at major junctions or turning points in the ministry of the Lord, almost as introductions and conclusions to highlight or typify portions of His work.

What is called "Higher Criticism" looks at the literary and historical content of the Bible. It asks questions about; the structure of the book, the date of authorship, and where the material came from (also known as source criticism). Higher Criticism claims to be scientific by using several denials or assumptions: 1) it rejects the Bible as Divine revelation, 2) it rejects miracles, 3) it rejects the resurrection of Jesus Christ, 4) it rejects predictive prophecy, 5) it rejects that Moses wrote the Pentateuch, 6) it rejects the Gospels are independent reports by four eyewitnesses, and it rejects that 7) Paul wrote the Epistles that are attributed to him. Higher Criticism begins with the view that there must be natural explanations for the quality and content of the Bible. Nothing miraculous or supernatural is allowed by "Higher Criticism."

Several conclusions are drawn from those assumptions. The first is that individual books of the Bible were written by several writers, at a later date then previously considered, or were compiled by a committee over time. Related to that is the theory that the law, which is so unique and advanced, must have developed and evolved over time. Also, there must be a natural explanation of each miracle, or else it was fabricated to use as a teaching device. Finally, anything recorded as being foretold in advance was actually written after the fact, as though it were a foretelling, in order to add supernatural credibility to the book. Higher Criticism claims the Bible is a myth, not literally true, perhaps well-intentioned, but still a myth.

To understand the exact nature and depth of this fraud it must be remembered that science is allowed to, even required to, make assumptions. Otherwise Higher Criticism would simply have been labeled unbelief and discarded. Instead it was welcomed (forced) into seminaries and universities and hailed as a scientific approach. Resistance was labeled anti-science. The rational was that by using and examining these assumptions a more complete understanding of Holy Scripture would emerge.

A scientific tool or experiment is neither true nor false. It is just a process. It is a good idea to use some systematic, scientific approaches when examining the Bible. Higher Criticism is not that. Despite its claims, it is really a wolf in a scientist's lab-coat.

An example of the scanty "evidence" used by Higher Criticism is the claim that the use of two different words; "Elohim" or "Yahweh" to refer to God in the Pentateuch, must indicate two authors. However, as early as the 8th century, the Midrash mentioned the observation of Rabbi Ben Azzai that when sacrifices are mentioned in the Pentateuch God is always called Yahweh. Other principles of Higher Criticism have been applied to ancient and contemporary writings and laws whose authors are well known. They erroneously "prove" that those works were written by several authors over time.

None of the assumptions of Higher Criticism, some which are almost 2,000 years old, have ever been supported. All the supposed evidence has fallen apart under examination. Higher Criticism has never produced any helpful information. It has been discredited by many prominent theologians and by both Christian and non-Christian scientists. These assumptions, that were supposed to be proven, and were supposed to be tools, or means to an end, were simply an end in themselves. That end was to discredit the Bible in the name of science. Its failure lends credence to a supernatural view of scripture but by some "miracle" it continues to be taught. It keeps getting brought up on university campuses because of the desire to hide disbelief behind the name science. As one science professor put it: "any alternative, even a bad one, is better than believing in God." Is it?

Higher Criticism, by virtue of its claim to be a scientific view of the Bible, became a mandatory position at many seminaries and universities. The work of Carl Jung and Joseph Campbell follows in the same so-called scientific tradition of rejecting the supernatural as myth. They pioneered the concept of the "psychological need of man for religion."

Joseph Campbell, in greater detail than Carl Jung, pointed out the common themes of myths and legends from different cultures. The theme of renewal; birth, death, and new birth, which also reflects the changing seasons, is one repeated theme. Heros and villains, good and evil, are two others. Shapes, such as circles, squares, triangles, pyramids, Xs or crosses, also appear in stories from different cultures around the world. They are all part of mankind's experiences. These ethnic studies show that we humans have much in common with each other no matter where we live or in what culture we are raised (Deut. 4:19).

The insupportable claim is added to these observations of common experiences that <u>all</u> religions are man-made and of equal validity. The claim is that all variations exist in our collective consciousness. This approach demands we study common themes in all religions *except* for claims of quality, or exclusive, divine revelation. The myth about myths, which Campbell promotes, serves to devalue and exclude the unique qualities of the Bible. Claims that it is unique are labeled unscientific and narrow-minded.

The revelation of the One, Just, Holy, and Personal, God, stands out in great contrast to other legends of plural, fickle, profane, indifferent, or otherwise occupied, forces or demi-gods. The explanations of events, and experiences, recorded in the Bible, whenever recorded or measurable by other means, have always been proven correct. The quality and accuracy of the Bible make it much more than a myth or legend.

Since no tool exits to measure the presence of God the claim is that the "rational" thing to do is just study man and reject anything that has to do with the supernatural. This is a bogus argument. Scientific studies of man would include the careful tabulation of the testimony of witnesses and the recording of events that have no explanation without assumptions of what must be excluded. The effects of God are knowable. It is a standard scientific practice to predict and theorize about the existence of some unknown or unmeasurable cause by measurement of effects.

The assumptions of Higher Criticism, and the use of myths as evidence that all religions are equal, are still a part of our culture. This may have reached a peak in 1966 when the question on the cover of TIME magazine was: "Is God Dead?" The supernatural revival and spread of churches that swept the nation, and the world, shortly after that, would seem to indicate the answer is no, but that is evidence that some scientists refuse to consider.

This next issue, misapplication of Systematic Theology, may be labeled the myth of the all-knowing theologian. It by-passes the question: "what does God's word say about a particular situation?" Instead, Systematic Theology attempts to examine a question or a theme thoroughly, using the entire Bible, to come up with a one size fits all, for all time, answer. This is misused on many topics but can be highlighted by looking at the study of salvation (Soteriology), a central issue, and prosperity preaching.

New Christians often run into the confusion generated by certain questions. We mistakenly believe that if a question is posed it can or should be answered. A question may be loaded or slanted, or need to go beyond the content, such as: "what is the sum of two apples plus three oranges?" The only answer is to use a <u>higher order concept or process</u> than that which is contained in the question. The answer can not be given as *either* apples *or* oranges but is five *pieces of fruit*.

One such question is whether salvation is by grace, requiring only faith in Jesus Christ, or by merit; requiring religious activities and good deeds (lumped together under the title of "works" or "effort"). The Bible teaches that certain works are the evidence or result of faith in Jesus Christ and other works are evidence of reliance on self, the world, or the devil. This is not an "either/or" contradiction nor an unanswerable double bind.

The higher order answer is that both faith and works go together. This is a mystery: "by grace are ye saved through faith;" "not of works," (but) "unto good works," this "mystery ...is Christ in you" (Eph. 2: 8-10, Col. 1:27). We may not like living with a mystery but not all questions have a simple yes/no answer. Faith in Jesus is the work of God (John. 6:29). It is also true that faith without works is dead (James. 2:17). The more important question is "why ask this question?"

The evangelist Charles Finney wrote, in Revivals of Religion, his approach to another related question: "can a believer lose his or her salvation?" At times he preached to people who were pressing on in God but were burdened and in spiritual warfare. He would uplift and encourage them by using those scriptures which dealt with the assurance of eternal security and victory. On the other hand, when he came to Christians who were smug in their attitude or lazy in the pursuit of God he would preach those scriptures which exhorted to diligence and warned of dire consequences for those who did not stay alert.

Both types of scriptures are in the Bible. They are not contradictions, nor ammunition for theological debates. This can be very important in the context of a study of Luther versus the Catholic church, or Arminianism versus Calvinism, or Anabaptists. The point is what is the context? The form of some questions and debates is good academics, but wrong, or out of place, or just not needed in other contexts.

Systems theory introduced this point of view to family counseling. The best way of resolving irreconcilable differences is to find some specific higher order answers. Much earlier, when Jesus was ambushed by some either/or, "forced choice" questions, he resorted to higher order answers such as: "render... unto God the things that are God's," and "he who is without sin... let him first cast a stone..." (Matt. 22:21, Jn. 8:7). **Love, Mercy, Faith, Grace, Spirit, and Eternity are higher order concepts. These may need to be applied in precise ways, not as theology, or vague, general platitudes.**

These types of religious lies; asking forced choice, loaded, or slanted questions, or leaving out essential context, should be well known and hated since the first one, "Yea, hath God said..?" (Gen. 3:1), caused such a disaster. The serpent split the same hairs: time and spirit, that many such questions do. The answer is not found in just certain scriptures, but in using the whole sword of God as He directs.

* * * * * * * *

Prosperity preaching has long been popular in the United States. Many here preach: "come to Jesus, it's easy, you will get all or anything you want." It is systematically developed by teaching on the theme of God's goodness and blessings to us, using the many scriptures that express this. Then, all scriptures are interpreted from that point of view. Any questions or failures are called sinful unbelief and doubt.

One example is the popular interpretation of the scripture: "For every beast of the forest is mine, and the cattle upon a thousand hills." (Ps. 50:10), as meaning: "I can have anything I want because my Father (God) is fabulously wealthy." That passage in its context is a warning from God which in America has been turned around to mean the opposite - a promise of unrestricted blessing (Jer. 5:30-31, 6:13-14, Matt. 24:11, Lk. 9:23, I Tim. 6:5). When the promised blessings do not come people are crushed. This may be called: "being enticed by their own lusts" (Ja. 1:14).

Counseling here requires rebutting false doctrines and teaching the truth. The tendency to interpret all scripture in only positive ways, in the name of encouragement and hope, may work instead as a process of denial. It says: "we have not done, nor can we do, any wrong, because all is forgiven." This effectively slams shut the door of repentance, forgiveness, and growth by refusing correction and failures, even mistakes (Prov. 15:10, I Jn. 1:8-10).

These misuses of scripture are easy to cure. It is a well known principle of Biblical exegesis that the meaning of a word or scripture should be discovered in relation to the context(s) it is found in. The meaning should flow from the way it is used in the Bible passage, and not contradict the text, or ignore other major themes in God's word. However, we desire a brief, easy to understand God, Bible and answers to the difficulties of life.

CHAPTER IV REVIEW

Someone may ask if it is possible to lose one's salvation. This does not require a systematic review of the entire Bible. A better response is to find out if temptation or sin are a problem. The issue is: "why does the person feel so fearful or removed from the Lord that he or she has to ask this?" If the question is about salvation by works or faith, the real issue is to look for evidence of faith and works, not either/or. It is often personal issues, including sinful behaviors, not doctrines, that need to be dealt with.

(Scripture Reference for Chapter IV)

pg. 41
Jn. 8:32 - And ye shall know the truth, and the truth shall make you free.

pg. 45 - Deut. 4:19 - ...thou seest the sun... moon, and the stars... which the LORD thy God has divided unto all nations...

pg. 48
Eph. 2: 8-10 - For by grace are ye saved through faith;... **(9)** Not of works... **(10)** For we are his workmanship, created in Christ Jesus unto good works,...

Col. 1:27 - ...the glory of this mystery... is Christ in you the hope of glory;

Jn. 6:29 - ...This is the work of God, that ye believe on him whom he hath sent.

Ja. 2:17 - Even so faith, if it hath not works, is dead, being alone.

pg. 49
Matt. 22:21 - ...Render therefore unto Caesar the things which are Caesar's; and unto God the things that are God's.

Jn. 8:7 - He that is without sin... first cast a stone at her.

Gen. 3:1 - ...Yea, hath God said, Ye shall not eat of every tree of the garden?

pg. 50
Ps. 50:10 - For every beast of the forest [is] mine, [and] the cattle upon a thousand hills.

Jer. 5:30-31, 6:13-14 - A... horrible thing is committed in the land; **(31)** The prophets prophesy falsely, and the priests bear rule by their means; and my people love [to have it] so:... **(13)** ...every one [is] given to covetousness; and from the prophet... unto the priest every one dealeth falsely. **(14)** They have healed... the hurt... slightly, saying, Peace, peace; when [there is] no peace.

Matt. 24:11 - And many false prophets shall rise, and shall deceive many.

Luke 9:23 - And he said to [them] all, if any [man] will come after me, let him deny himself, and take up his cross daily, and follow me.

I Tim. 6:5 - ...men of corrupt mind, who have been robbed of the truth and who think godliness is a means to financial gain. (NIV).

Ja. 1:14 - But every man is tempted when he is drawn away of his own lust...

Pro. 15:10 - ...he that hateth reproof shall die.

I Jn. 1:8 & 10 - **(8)** If we say that we have no sin, we deceive ourselves... **(10)** If we say we have not sinned we make him a liar...

Again, let me reiterate, it is not the task of Christian or secular counseling to correct the myths, lies, and denials we all live with. It may be important to consider if these are contributing to a person's problems. If so, it is also important to consider if a person is willing to give them up. Perhaps even more important is that a counselor self-reflect about his or her own myths, lies and denial – including denying the existence of God.

Pause and Reflect.

V - Lies And Denial

"If we confess our sins he is faithful and just to forgive us our sins..." (I Jn. 1:9).

A myth may consist of many falsehoods or distorted ways of viewing reality. It can take a lot of effort to create and maintain. A simple lie or denial may be sufficient for whatever purpose is desired. This chapter will point out several more common forms of lies and denial. These things are not usually called *pathological* or sick. They may stem from, or lead to, conditions which are.

Just about every group twists scriptures to prove or justify their doctrine or tradition (Matt. 15:6, & 23:23). There have been wars over the form of water baptism. Splits occur because of music in church, or women in ministry, or the gifts of the Holy Spirit. Unrelated texts are used to disallow any gifts at all. Others argue that one gift, *tongues*, is the required evidence of spiritual regeneration even though the Bible is silent on this claim. The Apostle Paul, in I Cor. 12:11, clearly notes that authority over the giving of spiritual gifts is in the hands of the Holy Spirit (...as he will) not in the hands of men. However, church government and authority ***is*** in the hands of men, which is what decides these issues. **Scriptural swordplay is rarely effectual counseling.**

Words and scripture verses can take on opposite or totally unrelated meanings. Even meekness and gentleness may get re-defined as strong-willed harshness. It should come as no surprise when a counselor or a person in counseling uses scripture to justify anything they do, or do not do.

It is not uncommon to find the doctrine of ultimate reconciliation in this country, contrary to the teaching of one judgement day with an eternal heaven to be gained, and an eternal hell to be avoided (Heb. 6:2 & 9:27). There are some who will vehemently assail the Trinity: Father, Son, and Holy Ghost, as being in opposition to a belief in One God (Matt. 28:19, Jn. 15:26, Deut. 29:29). Some people believe that if anything goes wrong someone must have sinned so they search for the culprit. There are those who consider the Bible irrelevant or out of date. Some have an image of God as being mean, punishing, or out of touch. There is confusion over the meaning of the "free" gift of salvation in light of the cost of Calvary, and specific rewards or crowns, in view of the sacrifices made by believers over the centuries.

There is a market mentality here. A recent Pope reduced sentences in purgatory by 3 years for reading the Bible for 15 minutes. This is a far cry from the excesses of selling indulgences that were part of the fuel of the Reformation. However, it is similar to many other marketing techniques used in the church today.

Trying to make the Kingdom of God submit to man may be a manifestation of our cultural mindset to control and dominate. This creates a religion of rules, or "cause and effect," rather than "the cross and repentance." The aim of this type of spiritual technology is similar to the aim of science; to control, but in this case the goal is to control the natural AND the supernatural. It may be simpler to attribute this to the fall of Adam and Eve, or a pampered people who assume they can get whatever they want. It could also simply be called pride, or the fear of death.

The purpose in mentioning these beliefs is not to suggest that people holding them do not or cannot also believe and live essential truths. Both religious and secular scientific frauds attract people with certain unhealthy motives. That these motives exist within the church community is important to consider in counseling. The Pentecostal historian, Bernard Bresson, wrote in Studies In Ecstasy (1966), "All religious groups attract those whose emotions can be moved upon by the Lord and this brings many who are emotionally unstable."

An individual or group may not be adhering to a religious variant because of their study of scripture. They may be driven to be right. They may have a need to be powerful, or perfect in order to overcome a past injustice or pain and to condemn the "other(s)" who wronged them.

It is not hard to discern when that is the motive for following a group or doctrine. What is being observed is not a new "revelation." It is a personality problem manifesting through religion. Clear simple truths are ignored for an extreme that promises to makes the believers even more "special." **Just correcting the theological error does not deal with the underlying cause(s) and will in many cases be ineffectual (Ro. 14:1).**

Extremism takes place in politics and with the fans of: sports heros, and movie, and rock stars. It should also be noted that soldiers, police, fire fighters, and medical personnel are called on, from time to time, to live and work outside of a safe, or "balanced" reality. Our nation was built by extremists who pledged their lives, fortune, and sacred honor for the ideals they believed in. Zealotry, being a fanatic, or even the denial of real conditions is not a problem unless the person, or those close to him or her, say it is. The difference between a hero and a lunatic may rest more with history than psychology (Matt. 12:33, Gal. 4:18). Many called Jesus mad or besides himself.

* * * * * * * *

A lie can become even more dangerous when it blocks the approach to salvation or to any help. One way this happens is the teaching that fear, worry, or doubt are sin. Under this old lie a problem can only be mentioned once when requesting prayer. After that the person must "believe" and have "faith."

Coming to a minister for help or comfort more than once for the same problem is called a sin of unbelief. This lie saves the pastor from being involved with a person's difficulties or being invited to what are scornfully called "pity parties." This is a sign of a toxic faith in churches that only use people for the profit, power, and prestige of the leader(s). Hurting people may be so needy that they put up with, and even expect as normal, such abuse. Secular counseling also has those whose practice is more exploitative than curative, just a job, but they are not disguised as messengers of God (II Cor. 11:14, I Pet. 4:17 & 18).

Much care is needed to heal and restore those who have been wounded by the hyper-faith teaching that only faith will help. Some very influential ministers have rejected compassion as being totally worthless. They may have only meant to emphasize faith, however, this contradicts the Bible (Heb. 5:2, Zech. 7:9 & 10, Matt. 18:33). One faith preacher sells a book on how not to lose your miracle and why people are not healed or do not stay healthy. He may have a gift (Ro. 11:29), but what he sells is more a form of "magic mind control" (Prov. 18:21, Matt.12: 34 & 37, Jer. 5:30-31, 14:14). A good attitude and words of hope can help, mentally and physically. However, we must discern the difference between spiritual power and the psychic or psychological realm. One very popular form of preaching in America is motivational speakers who inspire their listeners, whether in a secular or a Christian setting.

Misinterpretation can be taken to the point of fraud. We should not overlook the need for spiritual growth, nor ignore spiritual gifts or hope in miracles (Ps. 27:13, Heb. 11:6). However, when false spiritual laws are sold like lottery tickets for a blessing from God they turn "...the just shall live by his faith" (Hab. 2:4) into a technique for control and power, rather than a vehicle for living with God.

The book of Job explores this problem of a person in pain and distress being accosted by "friends" with vain religious platitudes (Job 16:2). Blaming the people who are hurting for being in pain and for not having the faith to get out of and stay out of pain is called by one pastor "the ministry of adding insult to injury." It is also what the Bible calls oppressing the poor (Pro. 22:22).

Our God, the Father of the Lord Jesus Christ, is a God of compassion (Ps. 86:15). He has pity on us as a loving father pities his children (Ps. 103:13). He identified with us, and joined himself to us, as a human being, in our failures, difficulties, and pain (Phil. 2:7). He is looking for pastors who have that same heart attitude (I Sam. 13:14, Jer. 3:15). He hates those who abuse his people, whether they are called counselors, or pastors, or teachers, or evangelists, or prophets, or apostles (Jer. 23: 1-4, Ezk. 34:10, Rev. 2:6).

* * * * * * * *

Denial goes hand and hand with lies and false teachings. It is a major block in counseling. The word denial gained popularity describing the refusal of alcoholics to admit they were drinking, that it was a problem, that they could not control it, and that they needed help. The denial is of the existence of a problem, or responsibility for it, and is often accompanied by an unrealistic hope and/or by blaming others for the damage which occurs.

The opposite of denial is confession. Adam's response when God exposed his disobedience was denial by blame shifting. "The <u>WOMAN</u> whom <u>THOU</u> gavest to be with me, she gave me of the tree, and I did eat." (Gen. 3:12). So was Saul's reply to Samuel when he shifted blame to "the people" (I Sam. 15:24). Later it was described by Freud as one of many ego-defense mechanisms.

The word denial has gained wider coinage to describe all refusals to face and deal with problems whether or not they stem from substance abuse or some other difficulty. For some the scriptures are laws to obey rather than graces to obtain. Using the Bible in a legalistic way can be a means of denial (II Cor. 3:6b, Mk. 2:27). So is the refusal to examine our own behavior (I Cor. 11:28). This may be done by refusing to change or by wearing a facade of "spirituality" and complete sanctification. Motives and feelings such as envy, jealousy, anger, selfishness, lust, meanness, fear, or competitiveness, are repressed and denied.

A child caught misbehaving may be asked why he or she did it. Instead of admitting to anger, envy, or some other "horrible" motive the culprit will stare at the floor and say "I dunno." Adults, answer with: "it was just poor judgement," or "an accident," or "I made a mistake," or "it was due to a lack of real understanding." We use sophisticated justifications, or say "life is not fair," or even say; "I dunno." We deny and hide our "darker" side sometimes to the extreme point of not being able to recognize our own motives. Jesus said go to the person with whom you have a problem, deal with it, do not hide it (Matt. 5:23-24, Eph. 4:25). Instead, we deny this and “just forgive.” God knows our hearts better than we do (Jer. 17:10).

It is a good idea to let each person confess and confront his or her own myths, lies, or denial. Confrontation may only lead to denial of denial or to a quick brush-off as to the seriousness of the problem. Most people know the problems they live with and create. They may also know how to live and resolve problems. It is not uncommon for a counselor to be presented with a catastrophe which quickly turns out to be the result of someone's lie or denial - which everyone involved with is aware of, but no one wanted to mention. Pastors and counselors may also get dragged into situations where a person just wants to profit, or that are not really crisis, but are the denial of normal discomfort. It is common to attempt to express as extreme the normal stress and difficulties of life.

Another common form of denial is denying hurt and painful feelings, or a refusal to express or allow the outward expression of feelings. This may be a cultural phenomenon. For many, however, it is the result of the long-time practice of repressing any emotions caused by pain or loss. Some take a scripture to extremes, such as II Tim. 1:7, or I Jn. 4:18, using it to forbid feeling any fear.

Certain groups have doctrines that extol joy and gladness and reject grief and sadness. No one is allowed to be sad at their meetings! If a person is unhappy they will be forced to sing and dance until they smile and laugh. Even when a real and serious reason for sorrow is known the solution is to repress the "bad" feelings and rejoice.

A central part of the Christian message is that Jesus endured the suffering, shame, and pain of the cross when He bore the punishment for the sins of all mankind. A first century heresy, Docetism, claimed the Lord's humanity was only apparent, that He was on the cross in spirit, not in flesh, and therefore did not feel pain. Anything to do with the flesh was considered evil. The goal then was to crucify the flesh. Another variation is the impassibility heresy that cannot conceive of God dying. This claims the God part of Jesus did not die. The "no pain and suffering" doctrine in America today demands long life, good health, and wants to pamper the flesh. It is only a slight variation of those earlier false teachings (Ecc.1:9).

This is not just heresy (Ecc. 3:4, & 7:3 & 4, Jn. 11:35, I Cor. 12:26). It is a formula for mental illness. It can lead to pathologies that are called dissociative disorders. They can be of external or internal reality, of the physical body, or any feelings, or even one's own identity. They are manifested on a continuum from simple memory loss to multiple personalities. As a response to trauma this process is a coping mechanism for emergency or crisis situations when it is better to ignore the pain or problem so as to work on survival. Because of it we are capable of "super human" efforts. As a lifestyle or doctrine it is dangerous and unhealthy.

* * * * * * * *

Many people simply do not want to admit there are problems for which we have no answers. A multiple sex offender in Texas wanted to be castrated instead of serving a life sentence in prison. A priest in Massachusetts, convicted on multiple counts of pedophilia, pleaded for a lenient sentence with counseling. Both these requests were denied. The fact is that neither has been shown to be an effectual way to stop this evil abhorrent behavior and to protect children. The group work, Parents United Inc., begun in 1971 by Dr. Henry Giarretto, does appear to work with certain "less severe" cases of child molesters, (that is, if the term "less severe" can be used at all here), but even after serving jail sentences and/or counseling, or after castration, many will commit this violent act again.

Chronic lying is another serious problem. A person or couple will ask for counseling with a complaint of "confusion" or sometimes it is called "doubt." After questioning and investigation, what emerges is a long held pattern of lies. It may be through hypocrisy, manipulation, myths, lies, or denial, half-truths, or a refusal to accept the truth. Some hidden secret from the past may be plaguing them, or it may be a secret life-style. Like moths around a lightbulb they circle the problem, never letting go of the lie. They will get burned.

One result of living a lie is confusion and losing the ability to know what is true. Another result is guilt, which turned outward may become anger, or when turned inward may manifest as depression. Extreme cases may result in symptoms of mental illness or even possession by a spirit of deception (II Thes. 2:10-12). **The counselor is wise not to try to untangle the web of deceit.** Part of the pattern is to create more lies. The person coming for counsel may be challenging the counselor to guess the secret or prove them wrong.

The solution is to cut the Gordian knot with the sword of truth. **Complete confession, and a renewed life that actively rejects duplicity is the goal.** A love of the truth, hating lies and all evil, and open confession with mutual accountability is the way to overcome this problem (Col. 3:9 &10).

It must be pointed out that confusion may be caused by many things such as: new situations, or being overwhelmed with too many choices, or by having contradictory choices. A classic case is the double bind: "I love you, eat, that's good," but "if you eat, you'll get fat, nobody will love you, that's bad." We all have to eat. A child bombarded with contradictory communication; with opposing conditions for love, learns appearance and food are factors that control love which they cannot control, though they may try very hard to control. He or she is caught in a bind and must rebel, go crazy, or find a higher order answer.

* * * * * * * *

Denial is so common and such a hindrance that it may be focused on with the belief that once it is broken a cure will follow. This is not always true. A person's denial can be exposed by: video or audio tape of his or her behavior, or by being confronted by the testimony of children, spouse, or friends. He or she can be tripped up in their own words and lies but may simply get angry, hostile, defensive, and leave and go right on with whatever the problem is. The counseling process may be repeated again and again with different counselors or churches until the person gets caught there too. Sometimes denial is exposed too soon or too harshly. When people get brutalized this way "for their own good," they may need help to recover from the counseling! For many people the process of change is difficult and threatening.

Chapter V Review

Has your theology been challenged by this last chapter? A group of hyper-faith missionaries was recently expelled from Russia. They went in proclaiming miracles. None occurred. As usual in America they blamed the people for not having enough faith and instructed them to believe more. The Biblical order is not to preach miracles, but to preach the Gospel; Christ crucified for our sins and risen again. Then signs and wonders follow.

Myths, lies, and denial seem like simple matters. What are: learning disorders, conduct disorders, and personality disorders? What about severe pathologies such as schizophrenia and other psychoses? Are these problems relevant to what you do? Do you have boundaries and know to say, “I cannot help.” The next three chapters are going to explore some theories and descriptions of mental illness. This is a good time to stop and consider what counseling problems you do face. How do you handle them? What myths, lies, and denial do you live with? How can the reality of God be compared with the many myths we live with?

There is a line in the song People Need The Lord which says: "We are called to bring His light, to a world where wrong seems right." The hymnist wrote in This Is My Father's World; "...O let me ne'er forget, That though the wrong seems oft so strong, God is the ruler yet!" The theme of Myths, Lies, and Denial is certainly not new.

(Scripture references for Chapter V)

pg. 53 - I Jn. 1:9 - If we confess our sins, he is faithful and just to forgive us our sins, and to cleanse us from all unrighteousness.

Matt. 15:6 & 23:23 - ...Thus have ye made the commandment of God of none effect by your tradition. **(23)** Woe unto you... for ye... have omitted the weightier [matters] of the law, judgement, mercy, and faith;

I Cor. 12:11 - But all these worketh that one and the selfsame Spirit, dividing to every man severally as he will.

pg. 54 - Heb. 6:2 & 9:27 - ...the doctrine ...of eternal judgement...**(27)** And as it is appointed unto men once to die, but after this the judgement:

Matt. 28:19 - Go... teach all nations, baptizing them in the name of the Father, and of the Son, and of the Holy Ghost:

Jn. 15:26 - But when the comforter is come, whom I will send unto you from the Father, [even] the Spirit of truth, ...he will testify of me:

Deut. 29:29 - The [secret things] belong to the Lord our God but [those things which are] revealed [belong] to us...

pg. 56 - Ro. 14:1 - Him that is weak in the faith receive ye, [but] not to doubtful disputations.

Matt. 12:33 - ...for the tree is known by [his] fruit.

Gal. 4:18 - But [it is] good to be zealously affected always in a good thing....

pg.57 - II Cor. 11:14 - ...for Satan himself is transformed into an angel of light.

I Pet. 4:17 & 18 - For the time [is come] that judgment must begin at the house of God: and if [it] first [begin] at us, what shall the end [be] of them that obey not the gospel of God? **(18)** And if the righteous scarcely be saved, where shall the ungodly and the sinner appear?

Heb. 5:2 - Who can have compassion on the ignorant, and on them that are out of the way; for that he himself also is compassed with infirmity.

Zech. 7:9-10 -...Execute true judgment, and shew mercy and compassions... **(10)** And oppress not the widow, ... fatherless, the stranger, nor the poor...

Matt.18:33 - Shouldest not thou also have had compassion on thy fellowservant, even as I had pity on thee?

Ro. 11:29 - For the gifts and calling of God [are] without repentance.

Pro. 18:21 - Death and life [are] in the power of the tongue...

Matt. 12: 34 &37 - ...out of the abundance of the heart the mouth speaketh. **(37)** For by thy words thou shalt be justified, and... thou shalt be condemned.

Jer. 5:30-31 & 14:14 - A ...horrible thing is committed in the land; **(31)** The prophets prophesy falsely, and the priests bear rule by their means; and my people love [to have it] so... **(14)** ...The prophets prophesy lies in my name: I sent them not ...they prophesy unto you a false vision and divination,... and the deceit of their heart.

pg. 58 - Ps. 27:13 - [I had fainted] unless I had believed to see the goodness of the Lord in the land of the living.

Heb. 11:6 - he that cometh to God must believe that he is, and [that] he is a rewarder of them that diligently seek him.

Hab. 2:4 - Behold his soul [which] is lifted up is not upright in him: but the just shall live by his faith.

Job 16:2 - I have heard many such things; miserable comforters [are] ye all.

Pro. 22:22 - Rob not the poor, because he [is] poor: neither oppress the afflicted in the gate...

Ps. 86:15, & 103:13 - But thou, O Lord, [art] a God full of compassion, and gracious, longsuffering, and plenteous in mercy and truth. **(13)** Like as a father pitieth [his] children, [so] the LORD pitieth them that fear him.

Phil. 2:5 & 7 - ...Christ Jesus: **(7)**...was made in the likeness of man.

I Sam. 13:14 - ... the LORD hath sought him a man after his own heart, and the LORD hath commanded him [to be] captain over his people, ...

Jer. 3:15, 23:1-4 - And I will give you pastors according to mine heart, which shall feed you with knowledge and understanding. **(1)**Woe be unto the pastors that destroy and scatter the sheep of my pasture! saith the LORD. **(2)** ... thus saith the LORD God of Israel against the pastors that feed my people; Ye have scattered my flock, and driven them away, and have not visited them: behold, I will visit upon you the evil of your doings... **(3)** And I will gather the remnant of my flock ... and will bring them again to their folds... **(4)** And I will set up shepherds over them which shall feed them: and they shall fear no more, nor be dismayed ...saith the LORD.

Ezek. 34:10 - Thus saith the Lord GOD; Behold, I [am] against the shepherds; and I will require my flock at their hand, and cause them to cease from feeding the flock; neither shall the shepherds feed themselves any more; for I will deliver my flock from their mouth, that they may not be meat for them.

Rev. 2:6 - But this thou hast, that thou hatest the deeds of the Nicolaitans, which I also hate.

pg. 59
Gen. 3:12 - ...The woman whom thou gavest [to be] with me, she gave me of the tree, and I did eat.

I Sam. 15:24 - ...I have transgressed ...because I feared the people, and obeyed their voice.

II Cor. 3:6 - Who also hath made us able ministers of the new testament; not of the letter, but of the spirit: for the letter killeth, but the spirit giveth life.

Mark 2:27 - And he said unto them, The sabbath was made for man, and not man for the sabbath:

I Cor. 11:28 - But let a man examine himself, and so let him eat of [that] bread, and drink of [that] cup.

pg. 60
Matt. 5:23-24 - Therefore if thou bring thy gift to the alter, and there remember that thy brother has aught against thee;
(24) ...go thy way; first be reconciled to thy brother, and then come and offer thy gift.

Eph. 4:25 - ...putting away lying, speak... truth...

Jer. 17:10 - I the Lord search the heart.

pg. 61
II Tim. 1:7 - For God hath not given us the spirit of fear, but of power, and of love, and of a sound mind.

I Jn. 4:18 - There is no fear in love...

Ecc. 1:9 - ...[there is] no new [thing] under the sun.

pg. 62
Ecc. 3:4 - A time to weep, and a time to laugh; a time to mourn, and a time to dance;

Ecc. 7:3-4 - Sorrow [is] better than laughter: for by the sadness of the countenance the heart is made better. **(4)** The heart of the wise [is] in the house of mourning; but the heart of fools [is] in the house of mirth.

Jn. 11:35 - Jesus wept.

I Cor. 12:26 - And whether one member suffer, all the members suffer...

pg. 63
II Thes. 2:10-12 - ...because they received not the love of the truth, that they might be saved. **(11)** And for this cause God shall send them strong delusion, that they should believe a lie: **(12)** That they all might be damned who believe not the truth, but had pleasure in unrighteousness.

Col. 3:9 & 10 - Lie not one to another, seeing that ye have put off the old man with his deeds; (**10**) And have put on the new [man], which is renewed in knowledge after the image of him who created him:

VI - Personality and Pathology

Part A - Basic Theories

"Train up a child in the way he should go: and when he is old, he will not depart from it." (Pro. 22:6).

Jethro suggested that Moses be for the people God-ward. Every great matter the people should bring to him. Every small matter should be left to others. What is the difference between a great matter and a small matter, a spiritual matter (God-ward) or a natural matter? Are all problems traceable to a root of bitterness, or to envy, anger, or jealousy? Are all problems due to the lust of the flesh, the lust of the eyes, and the pride of life? Are the categories we use all the time: sin and mental illness, or spiritual growth and character growth, or spiritual warfare and problems of life, mutually exclusive, or useful?

Gaining self-control and discipline, or getting rid of unclean habits, or self-centeredness should be a part of normal, healthy growth. This can be enhanced by a close relationship with Jesus Christ. It is helped by preaching, teaching, prayer, and God inspired will-power (Phil. 2:13) and by being part of a Christian community. Counseling may be personal witnessing dealing with: **sin** (Ro. 3:23, I Jn. 1:8, Gal. 3:22), and **salvation** (Jn. 14:6, Ro. 10:9), and **sanctification** (Eph. 4:14-15, 22 & 24, II Pet. 3:18, Acts. 24:25).

Personality and pathology can be expressed from a Biblical view of: the fall of man, sin, fear, pride, temptation, lust, rebellion, and disbelief (Mk. 7:21-23, Ro. 2:9, 14:23, I Cor. 6:9 & 10, Gal. 5:19-23). Basic Bible teaching and character studies try to do this. The Institute in Basic Life Principles is one attempt. "Biblical Counseling" may be used as a generic label for programs and training given at universities, or in church, and in mission seminars. Some systems, called Biblical, such as The Institute of Biblical Counseling, begun by Dr. Larry Crabb, borrow more heavily from psychology, as do the seminars of Gary Smalley, and others who are called Christian Psychologists.

The Christian Counselor's Handbook, used by the phone counselors at the counseling center of the Christian Broadcasting Network (CBN), among other places, is an indexed collection of problems and the Bible verses that relate to them. Another approach is The Christian Maturity Series, written by Paul Caram. This expounds on Biblical wisdom and teaches on the growth and development of the believer. The Secret of the Stairs, and Waterspouts of Glory, by Wade Taylor, describe spiritual goals and explore stages and methods of growth. The living gospel is still the greatest agent of change in the world. However, there are debates on whether change can or should be instantaneous, or gradual, complete, or partial. Application is open to debate.

The problems we face today have been with us since the fall of man. Envy, anger, and murder are found in the story of Cain and Abel. At that time a murderer complained that he would become a victim. He then got protection from retribution (Gen. 4:15). This is as new as today's headlines.

Whatever theory is believed will suggest what systems, goals, and techniques are used. The English have found that no system of counseling helps substance abusers. People simply grow out of it in about ten years if they survive. In England they provide drugs and clean needles to addicts. In France the disease model of alcoholism is not popular. For the French the goal is self-control, not abstinence. The very existence of a problem, and its severity, may be measured by: expediency, or by some cultural, social standard, or by a medical norm. An "appropriately" drunken, defensive, angry, fearful person may not be considered a sinner or sick.

* * * * * * * * *

Pastors may not have a system other than the Bible. They may simply be supportive, caring, and nurturing. The question "sin or sick" may never be raised. There are three main psychological views of personality and pathology: **1) learning and observable responses:** <u>Behaviorism</u>, **2) early conflicts in life:** <u>the psycho-dynamic model</u>, and finally, 3) **the meaning of life**: <u>Existentialism.</u> Each one has several versions and offshoots.

Two (over used) general terms need to be defined. **Psychosis** refers to a loss of, or a defective contact with **reality** such as being confused or out of touch in regard to self, place, time, or others. Believing in, or having contact with the supernatural is not a psychosis. **Neurosis** refers to **any other** disorder caused primarily by psychological factors.

The Diagnostic and Statistical Manual of Mental Disorders (DSM-V 2013) is based on behaviorism. This theory holds that personality and pathology are best described by listing observable responses or actions that have simply been learned. Behavior is only a function of its consequences. It will continue if it is reinforced (rewarded) by a pleasant stimulus, or by cessation of a noxious stimulus. It stops if it is discouraged (punished) by a painful stimulus, or by the loss of reward. This might be equated to: "He that spareth his rod hateth his son: but he that loveth him chasteneth him early." (Pro. 13:24, & 22:15).

People learn indirectly, such as by modeling or by vicarious experiencing (Phil. 3:17, Ecc. 8:11) or by more direct means. A comparison of learning theories and the Bible can be easily be made by looking at the way God has tried to teach and lead His people (Deut. 8:5, Heb. 12:5 & 6). The learning process and the use of reward and punishment is seen in the Bible. The principle is sound, but how we try to apply it is often questionable.

Both behavior learning theory and the Bible are used to justify the use of corporal punishment. Force may be applied too frequently and in circumstances where the emotional needs or habits of the parent control the situation rather than the learning needs of the child. Punishment may only teach a person to avoid the one who punishes, it may not change other long-term behavior or behaviors we want to change.

A behavioral approach does not ask "why" questions in regard to client history. It requires very precise information as to the: what, and when, for how long, and how frequently, and in what circumstances, a particular behavior occurs. The counselor tries to find, as much as possible, all the variables related to that behavior. By changing certain of those variables the behavior changes. This process works best with highly specific, unambiguous, short term goals.

This can, by a gradual desensitization, be an effective means to teach assertiveness, or it can deal with stress, obsessive compulsive behaviors, or phobias. It is used to help control impulsivity, relieve anger, or pain, and get rid of habits such as smoking. It is used to help with communication problems such as stuttering. Behavior modification even works well with children and adults who have little experience, or low intelligence, or cognitive limitation. Unlike other counseling processes it does not require a high degree of insight.

The earliest and still most popular theories of personality and pathology hold to the dominance of intrapsychic (within the mind) forces. A child will struggle with the external world and its own internal needs. During this struggle strategies are employed which become life-long habits. These are used to help him or her cope with the conflicts that emerge from living. The goal may be to seek pleasure, avoid pain, or to solve some other need.

The "dynamic" in the term psycho-dynamic means that personality is formed by these struggles which result in normal adjustment or pathology (Acts 8:23). Both internal and external forces, from the family, society, or all of human culture, interact within us. Different theorists suggest a variety of needs or motives for these struggles and describe an equally large variety of ways we learn to deal with them.

The issues, and methods of conflict, and the nature or types of defense mechanisms, roles, or personality structures, vary according to whose theory you read. Some of them are discussed in chapter VII. Freud is perhaps the best known theorist of causes of struggles in early life and the mechanisms that develop and are used throughout life. New motives or mechanisms for satisfaction are suggested from time to time. Psycho-dynamic theorists have to go to great lengths to define what it is they assume is going on inside a person since we cannot directly see inside.

Another modern theory as old as the Bible is the one behind Existential Psycho-therapy. This points out that with the collapse of reliance on traditional answers and cultural norms man is left with nothing to lean on to help him make sense of the world and his life. Without the answers given by religion we are faced with four basic conflicts. First, although mortal, we want to avoid death. Next, we are separate and feel isolated, but we do not want to be alone. Thirdly, although we are independent, we want to avoid responsibility for free choice. Finally, we require meaning but man will not accept arbitrary, authoritarian explanations. These four basic needs lead to others.

Mankind needs a meaningful framework to explain where we came from, why we are here, who we are, where are we going and how we get there. Without this, we refuse to accept: death, isolation, responsibility, or to find meaning in life, and we become removed from the immediate experience of living now. This leads to an inability to cope with living, To overcome this, therapists point out how clients avoid these issues such as by a reliance on external controls maybe by: being a slave to the clock, or a system, or a person. A client may avoid using the "I" and "my" personal pronoun. The therapist challenges the avoidance by saying: "you mean you won't," when someone says: "I can't." If someone spiritualizes, or denies owning his or her responses or feelings the therapist may ask: "whose feelings are they?"

When suicide is the presenting problem the short term process with this, or for any counseling, is intervention to resolve the immediate emergency. Hospitalization or detoxification may be required. Medical referral is a standard procedure for all counseling systems. The existential approach, with death issues or loneliness, over the long term, is to plunge into the feelings rather than attempt to reduce them. The person must deal with the major life questions that had been avoided. The question of eternal destiny often comes to the forefront once the reality of physical death is accepted.

What emerges in many cases is a story of childhood difficulty or crisis. This may have led to disappointment with God, or religion, and to the rejection of traditional answers. Both a Christian and a secular therapist could, at this point, agree that each individual must come to their own understanding of his or her mortality. They might both help, but from different perspectives. There is always a bias toward or away from the Bible. A counselor, and a culture, is never truly objective, but we can acknowledge this.

Raising any of these questions is a technique used by many evangelists. The solution to the problem of meaninglessness, which existentialists teach, is involvement with life. The Preacher in the book of Ecclesiastes discovered and shared this 3,000 years ago (Ecc. 9:4-10).

There are Christian existentialists, such as Soren Kierkagaard, and there are some people, like, Dr. Francis Shaeffer, who are very opposed to the psychology and philosophies practiced in their time. Dr. Shaeffer's antagonism to existentialism as he viewed it in the 50's and 60's was because he saw the asking of basic questions of values and existence as being a wedge designed to undermine Bible truths. Sixty years later our post-Christian culture is far removed from Biblical truth. The questioning of basic values today likely undermines the acceptance of the fallacies of secular myths and humanism.

An American college senior explained to a room of foreign students that Thanksgiving was a holiday in the United States to commemorate the time when the Pilgrims made a feast in order to give thanks to the Indians for their help. Everyone in the room knew this was false except for that student. Our culture, by way of the public schools, has been revised and rewritten. God, the Bible, and the Church, and our Christian heritage have been removed and are forbidden topics, even forbidden words in many places of our society such as school textbooks. Instead of prayer in schools we have guns and metal detectors. We also have a consumption economy which needs a Better Business Bureau to warn us against unprincipled merchants and now, because of serious malpractice problems, there is also malpractice insurance and a National Association Against Fraud in Psychotherapy.

Raising the four main existential questions: "What is the meaning of life?" (Ps. 144:3, I Cor. 6:19), "What is the meaning of death?" (Ps. 90:12, Acts 24:15, I Cor. 15:1-4, 26, Heb. 9:27), "Am I alone?" (Ps. 22:1, Jn 16:32, Eph. 2:19), and "What is my responsibility or purpose in life?" (Ecc. 1:1-18), does not undermine basic Christian values as Shaeffer feared because those values are no longer dominant considerations in western culture. Absolutes have been replaced with relative answers which are often unstable, dissatisfying, and false.

In summary, there are three major branches of counseling. Each approach has split into several variations. **(1)** Behaviorism is built upon theories of how we learn. It claims to only deal with those things that are observable or readily inferable. Behaviorists claim they can be more scientific this way. Sigmund Freud and other **(2)** psycho-dynamic or "depth" psychologists made inferences from clinical case studies about early childhood conflicts and needs. They focused on how those conflicts are resolved to meet basic needs. (3) Existential psychology focuses on the way an individual and their culture answers questions about life, death, purpose, aloneness, and authority. Inadequate answers lead to problems with living. These views can be found in scripture. However, the way they are used by a theorist, or a counselor, a church, a family, or an individual may differ greatly from the way the Bible deals with them.

Chapter VI Review

The questions raised at the beginning of this chapter were not answered because we cannot precisely compare sin, salvation, and sanctification with behaviorism, or psycho-dynamic, or existential psychology? Are these ways of viewing personality useful? The answer to that question may only come from each person's experience using these concepts. The issue remains as to whether or not all problems and answers are at their core spiritual, and what it means to be “worldly” or "God-ward."

If the focus is on resolving problems then the issue is what works best. Social scientists claim to know what sorts of families produce mentally ill people, or what sorts of social conditions produce wars. We still can not do much about either situation. What about the issue of a person's free will or choice? Psychologists claim to know how this is produced in someone. Theologians would point out that it is God who orders things in a person's life and conscience, even the intervention by a counselor.

The purpose of this book is to help pastors and counselors self-reflect by raising questions. Neither spiritual power, nor psychological technique is the main goal. Young David could not wear Saul's armor. God gave him the victory over Goliath with the weapon he was most comfortable using. A very basic concept we should keep in mind is the word:

Shalom: to be safe, healthy, happy, prosperous, whole, completed, full, restored, secure, at peace, and to have peace with God, through Jesus Christ, and the peace of God, and peace with one another.

(Scripture references for chapter VI)

pg. 71 - Prov. 22:6 - Train up a child in the way he should go: and when he is old, he will not depart from it.

Phil. 2:13 - For it is God which worketh in you both to will and to do of [his] good pleasure.

Ro. 3:23 - For all have sinned, and come short of the glory of God;

I Jn. 1:8 - If we say that we have no sin, we deceive ourselves, and the truth is not in us.

Gal. 3:22 - But the scripture hath concluded all under sin, that the promise by faith of Jesus Christ might be given to them that believe.

Jn. 14:6 - Jesus saith unto him, I am the way, the truth, and the life: no man cometh unto the Father, but by me.

Ro. 10:9 - That if thou shalt confess with thy mouth the Lord Jesus, and shalt believe in thine heart that God hath raised him from the dead, thou shalt be saved.

Eph. 4:14- 15, 22, & 24 - ...be no more children... **(15)** But speaking the truth in love, may grow up into him in all things, which is the head, [even] Christ: **(22)** That ye put off... the old man, which is corrupt according to the deceitful lusts; **(24)** - And that ye put on the new man, which after God is created in righteousness and true holiness.

II Pet. 3:18 - But grow in grace, and [in] the knowledge of our Lord and Savior Jesus Christ...

Acts 24:25 - And as he reasoned of righteousness, temperance, and judgment to come, Felix trembled, and answered, Go thy way for this time; when I have a convenient season, I will call for thee.

pg. 72 - Mk. 7:21-23 - for from within, out of the heart of man, proceed evil thoughts, adulteries, fornications, murders, **(22)** Thefts, covetousness, wickedness, deceit, lasciviousness, an evil eye, blasphemy, pride, foolishness: **(23)** All these evil things come from within, and defile the man.

Ro. 2:9, 14:23 - Tribulation and anguish, upon every soul of man that doeth evil... **(23)** ...for whatsoever is not of faith [is] sin.

I Cor. 6:9-10 - Know ye not that the unrighteous shall not inherit the kingdom of God? Be not deceived: neither fornicators, nor idolaters, nor adulterers, nor effeminate, nor abusers of themselves with mankind, **(10)** Nor thieves, nor covetous, nor drunkards, nor revilers, nor extortioners, shall inherit the kingdom of God.

Gal. 5:19-23 - Now the works of the flesh are manifest, which are: Adultery, fornication, uncleanness, lasciviousness,
(20) Idolatry, witchcraft, hatred, variance, emulations, wrath, strife, seditions, heresies, **(21)** Envyings, murders, drunkenness, revellings, and such like: of the which I tell you before, as I have also told [you] in timepast, that they which do such things shall not inherit the kingdom of God. **(22)** But the fruit of the Spirit is love, joy, peace, longsuffering, gentleness, goodness, faith, **(23)** Meekness, temperance: against such there is no law.

pg. 74
Pro. 13:24, 22:15 - He that spareth his rod hateth his son: but he that loveth him chasteneth him betimes. **(22)** Foolishness [is] bound in the heart of a child; [but] the rod of correction shall drive it far from him.

Phil. 3:17 - ...be followers together of me, and mark them that walk so, as ye have us for an ensample.

Ecc. 8:11 - Because sentence against an evil work is not executed speedily, ...the heart of ...men is... set... to do evil.

Deut. 8:5 - ...also consider in thine heart, that, as a man chasteneth his son, [so] the Lord thy God chasteneth thee.

Heb. 12:5 & 6 - And ye have forgotten the exhortation which speaketh to you as unto children, My son despise not thou the chastening of the Lord, nor faint when thou art rebuked of him: **(6)** for whom the Lord loveth he chasteneth, and scourgeth every son whom he receiveth.

pg. 76
Acts 8:23 - For I see that you are poisoned by bitterness and bound by iniquity. (NKJ version.)

pg. 78
Ecc. 9:4-10 - for to him that is joined to all the living there is hope: for a living dog is better than a dead lion. **(5)** ...the dead know not anything ... **(6)** ...neither have they any more a portion... **(7)** ...eat thy bread with joy ... **(8)**
...let thy garments be always white... **(9)** Live joyfully with the wife whom thou lovest... **(10)** Whatsoever thy hand findeth to do, do [it] with thy might; for [there is] no work, nor device, nor knowledge, nor wisdom, in the grave, whither thou goest.

pg. 80
Ps. 144:3 LORD, what [is] man, that thou takest knowledge of him! [or] the son of man, that thou makest account of him!

I Cor. 6:19 - What? know ye not that your body is the temple of the Holy Ghost [which is] in you, which ye have of God, and ye are not your own?

Ps. 90:12 - So teach [us] to number our days, that we may apply [our] hearts unto wisdom.

Acts 24:15 - And have hope toward God, which they themselves also allow, that there shall be a resurrection of the dead, both of the just and unjust.

I Cor. 15:1-4 & 26 - Moreover, brethren, I declare unto you the gospel which I preached unto you, which also ye have received, and wherein ye stand; **(2)** By which also ye are saved, if ye keep in memory what I preached unto you, unless ye have believed in vain. **(3)** For I delivered unto you first of all that which I also received, how that Christ died for our sins according to the scriptures; **(4)** And that he was buried, and that he rose again the third day according to the scriptures: **(26)** The last enemy [that] shall be destroyed [is] death.

Heb. 9:27 - And as it is appointed unto men once to die, but after this the judgment:

Ps. 22:1 - My God, my God, why hast thou forsaken me? [why art thou so] far from helping me, [and from] the words of my roaring?

Jn. 16:32 - ...I am not alone... the Father is with me.

Eph. 2:19 - Now therefore ye are no more strangers and foreigners, but fellowcitizens with the saints, and of the household of God;

Ecc. 1:1-18 - The words of the Preacher... **(2)** Vanity of vanities... all [is] vanity. **(3)** What profit hath a man of all his labour which he taketh under the sun? **(4)** [One] generation passeth away, and [another] generation cometh: but the earth abideth for ever. **(5)** The sun also ariseth, and the sun goeth down... **(6)** The wind goeth toward the south, and turneth about unto the north...and the wind returneth again according to his circuits. **(7)** All the rivers run into the sea; yet the sea [is] not full... **(8)** All things [are] full of labour... the eye is not satisfied with seeing, nor the ear filled with hearing. **(9)** The thing that hath been, it [is that] which shall be; and that which is done [is] that which shall be done: and [there is] no new [thing] under the sun. **(10)** Is there [any] thing whereof it may be said, See, this [is] new? ... **(11)** [There is] no remembrance of former [things]; neither shall there be [any] remembrance of [things] that are to come.... **(12)** I the Preacher was king over Israel... **(13)** And I gave my heart to seek and search out by wisdom... **(14)** I have seen all... and, behold, all [is] vanity and vexation of spirit. **(15)** [That which is] crooked cannot be made straight: and that which is wanting cannot be numbered. **(16)** ...yea, my heart had great experience of wisdom and knowledge. **(17)** And I gave my heart to know wisdom, and to know madness and folly... **(18)** For in much wisdom [is] much grief: and he that increaseth knowledge increaseth sorrow.

VII - Personality and Pathology

Part B - Structures and Patterns

"...put on the new [man], which is renewed in knowledge after the image of him that created him:" (Col. 3:10).

An underlying theme of psychotherapy is that we humans have, or are predisposed to have, certain mental structures or patterns. From this comes the idea that it is not the problems of life that need to be dealt with but rather our learned, maladaptive, excessive, or extreme responses to problems. Thus, malformed mental structures, bad answers, or ineffective strategies for coping with life are what are called "sick," or pathological. These are why a person's problems are psychological and appropriate for treatment by a psycho-therapist rather than by, or along with, someone from another helping profession.

Several theorists hold to the view that these patterns are self-regulating. They may have been shaped by childhood events but they are now maintained by a self-programming mechanism in the person's thought life. Words or mental images are endlessly repeated. This psychological theory has been adapted into a spiritual rule. Hyper-faith preachers and counselors seem to think they must constantly repeat their theme, almost browbeating their listeners, to move them from doubt to belief.

Dealing with doubt this way is similar to the practice of therapists who try to correct "negative thinking." The same kind of thought patterns are viewed, by both secular and Christian therapists, as being "sick," or "faulty." The goal is to find the basic and controlling thoughts and change the "tapes" to "reprogram" a person to think or handle life correctly.

Some people will make general statements that are negative or false such as: "all people are hostile or bad," or "life is dangerous." There may be false or impossible goals of security such as: "I must be rich," or "everyone must like me or else I'll be a failure." This may manifest as a dismal view of life such as: "life is so hard," "I can never succeed." A person may have the negative self view that: "I'm so stupid," or "I'm just a house-wife." Other faulty values include: "I must always win, even a single small mistake means failure." The list goes on and can be quite long.

These thoughts undermine a person's life and even their relationship with God. The faulty thought may be a religious concept. People may have been taught to believe that there is something wrong with them, or that God does not love them if they are not healed, or are not prosperous, or if they do not speak in tongues, or if they are not active in church. The aim is to produce faith but since not everyone is healthy, wealthy, or gifted, what is produced instead may be something else, such as guilt or estrangement.

Another popular way to view personality is in terms of consistent behavior patterns known as "roles." Dr. Alfred Adler looked at the roles due to the birth order of siblings within the family (oldest, middle, youngest). Virginia Satir pointed out other roles in a family. A "placater" is weak, passive, and readily agrees with others. There is a "blamer" who is self-righteous; and a finger-pointing, disruptive fault finder. The "irrelevant" one is often involved with distracting behavior without consideration of self or others in the immediate context, (perhaps glued to a smartphone). The "super-reasonable" person is devoid of feelings. That role is: intellectual, rigid, logical, and computer-like. Her label of a healthy role is "congruence;" where words and feeling match, without denying self, others, or the influence of the context.

The roles of the alcoholic family are the most well known. Family members trapped in these roles are cut off from their own feelings and needs just as much as is the substance abuser. These roles may describe families with other problems, not just substance abuse. There is the one "dependant" on alcohol (or drugs, or gambling). The "co-dependent" is addicted to the unhealthy relationship and may also be the "enabler" who helps to keep the ship afloat. The "hero" does everything well so as to hide the mess and pain of the family. The "scapegoat" acts out and gets the blame for the problems. The "clown" tries to make everyone laugh. The "lost child" is simply ignored, and the "rebel" leaves.

The view of Eric Berne, in his system "Transactional Analysis," is that we learn roles as children to use for the sake of attention. The roles he describes are: the "critical parent" (blaming), the "nurturing parent" (comforting), the "adult" (logical), the "free child" (creative), or the "adapted child" (conforming). James Framo describes roles as "object relations" from the family of origin. These are roles we viewed in others when we were children but now fear, want fixed, or still need, in our present relationships. This is a concept used in Harville Hendrix's "Imago-Relationship Therapy."

When stereotypical roles are evident it is a clue that the conditions which create(d) them are (or were) present. This may help in discerning a family's situation. One goal of role analysis is to help people break free of habitual roles and get in touch with, and express, their own emotions and needs apart from the roles they were forced into.

* * * * * * * *

Abraham Maslow created a "need" hierarchy which describes life in four "stages." He believed that in order to move on to a higher need, such as love, a more basic need, such as safety, has to be met. Erik Erikson described development in eight stages of growth. Other theorists have described the growth or stages of communication skills. There are theories on stages in the development of societal or personal morality and stages of "psycho-spiritual" development.

The point for counselors to consider is: what is the appropriate goal for the client according to whatever role or stage seems to apply to the presenting problem? How can the person get there? Training, or some kind of compensation, may need to be created or found.

Some theorists describe appropriate mental stages of development we go through in life. Jean Piaget reported four stages of cognitive (intellectual), development between birth and 12 years of age. Not everyone goes through these stages at the same age or to the same degree. If there is a severe discrepancy; a lack, or a regression from an advanced stage to an earlier one, this may indicate an emotional or an organic problem.

There are certain specific learning disorders (S.L.D.), such as Dyslexia, or Attention Deficit Disorder (A.D.D.). In addition to the problems resulting from a failure to learn, these can cause other personality and/or adjustment difficulties. Learning disabilities are not obvious to the casual observer. A person may learn early in life to hide their inability to read, do math, concentrate, or do other tasks necessary for learning to take place. School failure is a major cause of low self esteem. Timidity, shyness, and a resentful attitude are also the common products of this. Our ability to deal with, or diagnose, learning disabilities is still new.

Learning disabilities may lead to inefficient learning strategies which result in school failure and low job productivity. Many individuals with learning disabilities *do not use* the knowledge or strategies they have. They are correct in claiming that they *know* the material or the answer. They just cannot readily or easily use it. There may not be a lack of experience or intelligence as with cognitive limitations.

A person with a specific learning disorder may have an average, or even an above average score on an I. Q. test. The inability to strategize, or organize, or memorize, and execute tasks, is what often leads to failure. Persons with learning disorders need specific help learning what the majority of the population picks up incidentally.

The characteristics of people with an S.L.D. are that they may, in a much more pronounced manner than the general population, demonstrate frustration and respond impulsively. They appear to lack the ability to concentrate on any one thing for more than a short period. They are frequently smart, inquisitive, and eager to please but are also demanding, obsessive, and dependent. Less severe cases are usually not recognized. The majority are identified by their repeated failures in reading and mathematics however, on closer examination other deficiencies are usually noted. They may be verbally or physically abused by parents, siblings, teachers, and bullies.

Children are diagnosed with S.L.D. because it shows up in school. Adults who have a learning disorder share their symptoms. They demonstrate deficient, or distorted, social perception, and social competence, including a lack of self-control due to emotional interference. Their performance anxiety is high and non-participation is used as a coping mechanism. Their experience has taught them that success is dependant upon external factors rather than from their own internal strengths. They may exhibit helplessness by demanding supervision. Also common is low self-esteem including lack of motivation and feelings of inadequacy. These traits add up to failure: at school, work, and socially. Such descriptions are more precise than Paul's call to "comfort the feeble-minded" (I Thes. 5:14). **However, this may also be a by-product of our stressful educational system, and our fear, pride, and jealousy due to excessive competitiveness?**

The Diagnostic and Statistical Manual of Mental Disorders (DSM) has categories for the more obvious misbehaviors. Disruptive behaviors of children and adolescents are listed under the heading Oppositional Defiant Disorders. These are hostile, negativistic, and defiant behaviors. Those behaviors which violate the rights of others are called Conduct Disorders. These include: stealing, lying, running away from home, truancy, cruelty to people or animals, initiating fights, initiating forced sexual activity, or destroying property.

The DSM describes certain problems in adults using the classification Personality Disorder. These categories refer to long held patterns of behavior which may begin in adolescence or young adulthood. They might be called character flaws, personality differences, or odd, eccentric behavior.

The following disorders, and their prevalence, (shortened and paraphrased here), are examples of what is found in The Diagnostic and Statistical Manual of Mental Disorders (DSM-IV, 1994):

Paranoid (estimated .5% to 2.5% of the population.) A person with this disorder will rarely seek help because everyone is looked on with suspicion. This type tends toward moralistic grandiosity, they are punishing, disdain weakness and the weak, and have no real sense of humor. A cult leader could be diagnosed with this type of disorder. They tend to consider the actions of others as being deliberately demeaning or threatening. They expect to be harmed or exploited, They are easily slighted and quick to react and counter attack. They bear grudges and do not confide in others. They doubt the loyalty or trustworthiness of others. Saul versus David is one example even though Saul's fears of loss were real.

Schizotypal (3%), they have deficits in inter-personal relatedness, peculiarities of ideation, appearance, behavior, speech, and may hold odd beliefs. They feel extreme discomfort in normal social situations, and make inappropriate emotional responses.

Anti-social (2%), physically cruel and destructive, no sense of guilt, unable to conform to social norms in regard to work, finances, and honesty, is reckless and irresponsible, is often criminal. Being labeled with a P.D. does not exempt anyone from penalties.

Borderline (2%), shows an instability of: mood, self-image, and interpersonal relationships, chronic boredom, emptiness, takes extreme action to avoid abandonment, usually has many failed attempts at therapy. This is a catch-all diagnosis similar to low self-esteem, poor self-image, and co-dependency.

Histrionic (2% - 3%), displays excessive, extreme attention seeking and emotionality. They must be the center of attention, and are overly concerned with physical attractiveness. (Self-centered, proud, vain.)

Narcissistic (1%), these are hypersensitive to the evaluation of others but react to criticism with feelings of rage, shame, or humiliation, They have a sense of entitlement, self-importance, and act in a grandiose manner. They lack empathy, take advantage of others, and require constant attention.

Avoidant (.5% - 1%), avoids social contact unless certain of being liked, fears negative evaluation by others, has few or only one friend, exaggerates difficulty of doing anything outside of the routine.

Dependent (most frequent in mental health clients), is dependent, submissive, unable to make decisions, and fearful: of being alone, or of being abandoned. inflexibility, and a preoccupation with minor details

Obsessive-compulsive (1%), relies on rules or acts to control an internal rage by a perfectionism, that often obstructs task completion or enjoyment. They demand their own precise ways of doing things, and have restricted expression of affection.

Passive-aggressive (also Negativistic P.D.), is often sullen, irritable, impatient, argumentative, cynical, skeptical and contrary. Employs passive resistance to demands by: procrastination, going slow, making mistakes, or claiming to have forgotten. They resent suggestions on how to be more productive, obstruct the efforts of others by not participating, are very critical of people in authority, and often claim they are being misused.

People with Personality Disorders may have high scruples but be low on love. may have great vocational success but get little enjoyment in life. They may produce a lot, and be valuable employees, but they can become obsessed with unimportant details. A person may have more than one P.D., or parts of several. These tendencies can be observed in almost anyone but the diagnosis of a Personality Disorder requires an in-depth evaluation. These refer to a lifelong style of relating and a cluster of symptoms, not discrete episodes. There is usually a history of severe early childhood abuse. Dysfunctional family behaviors and the damages they cause are well known, though each person's response may be somewhat unique. These traits can also be learned as habits and passed on from one generation to the next.

The DSM uses different categories for children and adults because the personality of a child is not fully developed. Misbehavior must continue for six months to be labeled a Conduct Disorder. With adults, a pattern exits for a year or more before it is called a Personality Disorder.

Another common DSM structure, or syndrome (pattern of behaviors), counselors look for is: **Post Traumatic Stress Disorder**. The four symptoms of P.T.S.D. are: 1) a sudden re-experiencing of the trauma, 2) a psychic numbing - such as feelings of not belonging, or of being detached from all emotions, and 3) hyper-vigilance - always being anxious and poised for disaster, being a very light sleeper, constantly checking out how other people behave in order to be safe by following the rules of the present social interaction, and finally 4) survivor guilt - the feeling that they must fix things or that things must be fixed. This disorder, first described in combat veterans, was originally called shell shock or combat fatigue and is better known due to our many wars.

Additional insight into how we respond to extreme situations has also come from survivors of the holocaust like Corrie Ten Boon. The work of those caring for former prisoners of war, and torture victims and their families, such as Amnesty International, has also gone into this analysis. Faith stands out as a major factor in survival during and after extreme trauma.

The National Association of Adult Children of Alcoholics (N.A.A.C.O.A.) uses P.T.S.D. to describe people who grew up in abusive, unstable, alcoholic families. Survivors may have no idea what is wrong. They may recreate in the present, without alcohol, the situations they grew up with.

The characteristics of adult children of alcoholics are: 1) fear of losing control; this may look like pride, having all the answers, and always being right, 2) fear of feelings; which inhibits all talking about feelings, 3) fear of conflict; which hinders any efforts at compromise or negotiation, 4) an over-developed sense of responsibility; which may propel them into positions of leadership but not let them share responsibilities or make any mistakes, 5) an inability to relax and have fun; they carry the burdens of the world on their backs but may not want to, or even know how to, play with their own children, 6) feelings of guilt; God's grace is insufficient for them or anyone else; they find, or make up, rules and rituals to follow to appease their guilt, 7) intense self-criticism; this is more than a poor self-image, they have a life long habit of being criticized, 8) there is a confusion between love and pity; they refuse the help of those who care for them and they do not know how to give or show love, and 9) there is a fear of abandonment, they may go to extremes to maintain a relationship as a means of recovery.

One person may not exhibit all these traits. Each point may resemble something else, such as a Personality Disorder, or character flaw, or sin. This self-defensiveness may seem more like offensiveness. These are habitual defense postures and involuntary responses to past real danger. A.C.O.A.s learned early in life, by fear and shame, to repress the memory of the trauma; to hide "the secret" of the abuse and dysfunction of the family.

Richard Ganz, the psychiatrist who wrote Psycho-Babble, (1993), has suggested that looking inwardly at the past to fix a poor self-image may be what the Apostle Paul warned against doing in II Tim. 3:2 "For men shall be lovers of their own selves... ." Conversely, John Bradshaw, a former divinity student, in his books and TV series on the dysfunctional family, insists "the secret" of family abuse must be exposed. Otherwise the hurts go unhealed and the patterns get repeated.

Somewhere outside these extremes lies the truth. A person with a slight scratch may yell and complain just as loud or louder than someone with a broken leg. We tend to judge a person's pain and justify or condemn their response to it by our own experience. We may be wrong. Introspection and open expression are tools of counseling that are Biblical. Cases can be found to support or discredit both of the above points of view. It is our desire to help and our need for help that makes us try to help.

We all tend to be self-absorbed. Healing or growth is hindered by too much inward looking. Looking outwardly to Jesus is always good. However, recovery, like repentance, begins by admitting the need. That alone may not be enough to lead to needed change. It is often just the beginning of a lot of hard work. Help for any problem may only be available to those who pay the price in effort, time, and money.

Things may have to transpire on a spiritual and a natural level for healing to take place, both for the counselors and the ones being counseled. Self-centeredness (and burnout) is also manifested by the attitude that: "my problems and past are as bad, or worse than yours," or "I deserve as much special attention as you." No one was prepared for what they found in the concentration camps. Social workers are often overwhelmed with what they find when visiting a home. Someone may think a diaper rash is a serious problem if they have never been to a hospital pediatric intensive care unit. The reverse happens too. Mild or normal labels get put on severe conditions. One manifestation of self-protection is the denial of degrees of severity of problems.

The Bible notes the kinds of self-protection people go through in crisis. We often do not notice these in ourselves when a disaster is happening to us. Gently pointing these out is one helpful thing a friend, family member, or counselor may do.

The processes of hurt and recovery are patterns of personality we all share. Human beings are fallible and able, ruthless and compassionate. We all cause hurt, and get hurt. Problems, such as the personality and behavior changes associated with Alzheimer's disease, traumatic brain injury, strokes, cognitive impairment, or other "organic" conditions, are not helped by looking at "deep" causes. Some counselors focus more on how we survive, heal, and get on with life. One way is by focusing on functional ability and possibility rather than on limits and liability. Whenever possible, the environment needs to be examined so as to deal with more than just thought processes or "psychological" needs.

Often people seek help because they are faced with situations so unusual and drastic that no response they make is sufficient. Their coping skills are overwhelmed. They need to learn new coping skills to manage, tolerate, or reduce, the stress of trauma. Another tact counselors may take is that of a service brokers who direct people to the various services they need or they may provide direct care and supervision. Crisis and tragedy often force us to learn new patterns or techniques for living. A counselor may teach someone how to live with a problem which is not going away and may even get worse. The goal is to maximize remaining functional capacity and to minimize the limiting effects of a crisis or a disability or disabling situation.

Sometimes we are forced to adjust our old ways of looking at ourselves and our world. Both the self and social image and lifestyle may be effected by a disability. Dependency may increase. The whole family may need emotional support. Faith and church can be an anchor during such times and a resource for sharing information and resources on processes, services, and techniques used to deal with a disabling condition or situation.

To finish off the section on structures and patterns it will help to look at what we know about particular human responses relating to loss, pain, grief, and suffering. The following descriptions from Elizabeth Kubler-Ross (1974) and Hanoch Livneh, (in Marinelli & Dell Orto, 1991) and others, seem more precise than the poetry of the Psalms or the book of Job. Often however, it is in counseling or preaching from the Bible, or from contemporary scenes, that pastors will make just such elaborations by drawing on their own emotional experience or empathy.

It may take two or more years to mourn the loss of a spouse. Some things, like the loss of a child, may take five years or more to finally "get over" or grieve. Many people never do recover. Some tragedies are so severe that it is reasonable to consider that healing may not come this side of heaven or short of a miracle (I Thes. 4:13-18) with or without support from others. We can still try and may lesson the suffering, without ever healing or fixing the problem completely.

Bereavement literally means to be robbed. This loss of a loved one, or of functioning, or of our peace, is painful and we grieve over the loss. Although each person will respond, or not, in a unique way and time, the work of grieving can be described by stages. First comes initial awareness; being stunned, feeling guilt or self-blame, panic, and perhaps, but not always, denial. Next comes the search for strategies to cope. This may seem to be confusion between holding on and letting go (of an activity, or of a deceased person), or difficulty in making decisions. This may appear to be denial but may better be described as unfamiliarity with the situation (Job 10:15). A deeper awareness may include resentment, cynicism, sadness, anger and loneliness, which may manifest as exhaustion, self neglect, and lowered resistance to infection.

The healing process and the form or degree of expression of an individual's pain will depend on such things as: 1) the nature of the loss, 2) the degree of the attachment, 3) the amount of change in the daily routine, 4) the normal ability to cope with stress, 5) the support system that exists, and 6) having the permission and freedom to grieve. Two medical examples can help express the importance of this last point. When we do not grieve, or do not allow others to grieve as they choose, it may be likened to a wound that is infected which will than have to be re-opened and drained, or a broken bone that was incorrectly set that has to be re-broken and re-set in order to heal without restriction of movement and strength.

Freud elaborated on the insight of others when he theorized the existence of these eight ego-defense mechanisms: 1) compensation - working harder in a different direction with what strength is left, 2) denial - denying the existence of any problem completely, or 3) displacement – shifting feelings from an appropriate, unobtainable source to an accessible but inappropriate person or object, 4) introjection - incorporating the values of another, 5) projection - denying some disliked characteristic in oneself and assigning it to another person, 6) reaction formation - doing exactly the opposite of what is felt, 7) repression - banning unacceptable thoughts or feelings from one's consciousness, and 8) sublimination - modifying an unacceptable impulse into acceptable, or appropriate channels.

More obvious responses to severe pain and loss are well known by those exposed to it or by those who deal with people who are, or have been suffering. For people never exposed to grief or pain these may come as a shock. Our society tends to hide the sick, imperfect, and dying so ignorance of these responses is too common. These include: anger, blaming and guilt, attempts to control, bargaining (with God, or self, or others), self-abuse up to and including suicide, obsessiveness, argumentativeness, retaliation or bitterness, temper tantrums, striking out, abusive language, running away, and also substance abuse.

There may be periodic uncontrollable crying or screaming. Rebelliousness, unfocused fear, a sense of helplessness, depression, and withdrawal are other symptoms. These may occur at a much later time, even many years later, than the actual hurtful incident in what is referred to as Post Traumatic Stress Disorder or Trauma Syndrome. Delayed responses may be all that are possible (Ps. 77:4, Matt. 2:18).

We often fail to recognize these defense mechanisms or symptoms as part of the healthy, normal, grieving process. We may feel guilty for being "such a baby," or for being weak and out of control when others seem to be dealing with their problems with less difficulty. Tears and frustration are a part of bereavement but over time these will come with less intensity and frequency. Healing may come with self-understanding and acceptance. Further resolution comes when the need to blame is no longer present and some measure of joy can be experienced. Forgetting may never be possible.

The final transcending of the loss comes when it is possible to trust self and others again - or learning to trust for the first time. Some people have undergone many, unresolved, and ungrieved tragedies which makes dealing with the latest one all the more difficult (Job 10:1). Our response to a present loss may be based on the accumulation of all our responses to loss over our entire lifetime.

If the grieving process is thwarted healing may never come. There are cases where a pastor has rebuked the spirit of grief and ordered a deeply wounded person to repent and accept the joy of the Lord. Such spiritual warfare may at times be the proper course of action. A person may be under a spiritual oppression or be engaging in excessive self-indulgent mourning. However, in many cases, those who use this approach have themselves had severe and deep wounds that were never resolved and they may be unable to, or not know how to, deal with grief (Job 21:34). Several suggestions on dealing with grief are included in chapter IX on counseling techniques. Not grieving may cripple or kill a person. This is still a difficult topic to deal with. Our culture has a strong taboo against talking about death and tragedy.

The Bible, on the other hand, is very explicit about death and suffering. Those who only focus on joy, victory, and pleasant experiences are cutting out much of scripture and cutting themselves off from the grace of God. God's grace to help a person through grief includes His peace, strength, wisdom, and most of all, a very strong awareness of His presence. Some claim to have this grace when they are really dissociating, or using denial, repression, or some other defense mechanism. This is as damaging as a person claiming to be saved when they are not. It blocks or hinders the move toward true grace or any other kind of help.

Often periodic counseling is required during holidays or on the birthday of the deceased. The loss of what was expected but not realized such as: retirement activities, or travel, graduations and grandchildren, may need to be grieved as part of the "work of grieving." Grief is a normal response to any loss. Things that bring to mind the loss may cause pain. A caring friend or counselor can be helpful during such times. Faith helps, but rarely is anyone ever really prepared for such events.

A person might get stuck in one stage of grieving for a long time before he or she moves on - if they ever do. We each have our own cross to bear. How we bear it cannot be forced on others when we try to help them bear their own burdens (Gal. 6:2 & 5). The goal is to help a person through the natural, God given, healing process, and to help him or her find specific grace from God. Another goal is to simply be there and be supportive during grieving. Paul put it this way: "Rejoice with them that do rejoice and weep with them that weep." (Ro. 12:15 and I Cor. 12:26.)

Chapter VII Review

Many Christian systems present structures, roles, patterns, and stages using Biblical images and vocabulary. Putting on the "new man" is one. The "crucified savior," or "wounded healer," are Christian images used in more than one way. Think about some of the categories or labels you have heard or use.

Growth may be described using a Bible character such as: "the repentance of David," or "the recovery of Peter." Processes may be detailed but be labeled in terms of; "the road to Calvary," "the stations of the cross," or "the climb up Mount Zion." Character development has also often been described using animals. Some examples are: the courage of a lion, the single eye of a dove, or the wisdom of an owl. How are these collections of character traits and behaviors the same or different than the roles, stages, or processes described by psychology. Why or how are any of them useful?

The use of images and vocabulary that we are familiar with is a good way to communicate. If they are too familiar, or general, they may instead be easily ignored. A person may have repeatedly heard of the humility of the lamb and still refuse to repent or hold to a lie from the popular culture such as: "love means never having to say you are sorry."

Educational programs are also sold using Christian vocabulary. They may imply that the program is returning something special the public schools removed. Recently the courts ordered a phonics program to cease implying it was an effective tool for persons with learning disorders. It was similar to many others but it cost ten times more. Much of the cost went toward paying for expensive advertising through the Christian media.

Counselors may help someone see the things he or she is going through, and why. They may describe the way a person is responding or acting, and why. That does not automatically mean the person will change, or find healing.

> Psychology says: "ye shall gain insight and the insight shall make you free." The heart issues of motivation and direction in life, which God deals with, may be far more important. Jesus said: "And ye shall know the truth and the truth shall make you free." (Jn. 8:32), The "truth" that Jesus is referring to is more than mere accurate descriptions or facts about human life.

(Scripture References for Chapter VII)

pg. 87
Col. 3:10 - ...put on the new [man], which is renewed in knowledge after the image of him that created him:

pg. 93
I Thes. 5:14 - ...comfort the feebleminded, support the weak...

pg. 99
II Tim. 3:2 - For men shall be lovers of their own selves, covetous, boasters, proud...

pg. 102
I Thes. 4:13-18 - But ...concerning them which are asleep, that ye sorrow not, even as others which have no hope. **(14)** ...Jesus died and rose again, even so them also which sleep in Jesus will God bring with him. **(15)** ...that we which are alive [and] remain unto the coming of the Lord shall not prevent them which are asleep. **(16)** For the Lord himself shall descend from

heaven with a shout, with the voice of the archangel, and with the trump of God: and the dead in Christ shall rise first: **(17)** Then we which are alive ...shall be caught up together with them in the clouds, to meet the Lord in the air: and so shall we ever be with the Lord. **(18)** ...comfort one another with these words.

pg. 103
Job 10:15 - ...[I am] full of confusion...

pg. 105
Ps. 77:4 - ...I am so troubled that I cannot speak.

Matt. 2:18 - ...a voice heard, lamentation, and weeping, and great mourning, Rachel weeping [for] her children, and would not be comforted, because they are not.

Job 10:1 - My soul is weary of my life; I will leave my complaint upon myself; I will speak in the bitterness of my soul.

pg. 106
Job 21:34 - How then comfort ye me in vain, seeing in your answers there remaineth falsehood?

pg. 107
Gal. 6:2 & 5 - Bear ye one another's burdens, and so fulfil the law of Christ. **(5)** For every man shall bear his own burden.

Ro. 12:15 -Rejoice with them that do rejoice, and weep with them that weep.

I Cor. 12:26 - And whether one member suffer, all the members suffer with it; or one member be honoured, all the members rejoice with it.

VIII - Juxtaposition of Theorists

"The heart is deceitful above all things, and desperately wicked: who can know it?" (Jer. 17:9).

This chapter will attempt to compare some secular and Christian theorists. It is not possible in a brief overview to explore each one thoroughly. Simple broad snapshots of several theorists will be used to highlight some of the similarities and differences. Most contemporary counseling approaches combine parts of the theories already mentioned. What will work to cause change? The focus may be on a person's present thinking, feelings, or behaviors. It may help to explore past or future experiences or situations.

One of the reasons for writing this book was that almost all other counseling books seem to have too narrow a slant. The authors point out specific errors and real problems with psychology or with certain theorists, without explaining what it is the counseling is trying to get at in the first place. These "straw men" are easily blown away to prove that the new system, proposed in their current book, is true, that it works, and that it is Biblical. Myths, Lies, and Denial is not a new system. It is an attempt to describe the entire field so that pastors and church counselors can reflect upon the problems they see and the work they do and the involvement they may have with others.

That which is true in psychology, based on honest science, does not contradict the Bible. In fact, it originates from the Bible. The scripture references are provided in each chapter to help illustrate this (Eph. 4:14). One purpose of this book is to point out those scriptural roots in order to help readers develop discernment, not adopt a new system.

A strong connection exists between religious and secular counseling. An antagonistic example is the expressed purpose of Dr. Sigmund Freud, founder of the method known as "Psychoanalysis." He sought to create a "scientific" alternative to what he called "superstitious religions." That charge is not new. During the Reformation “superstition” was exposed and rejected. But Freud believed religious conversion was neurotic. Dr. Carl Jung, founder of "Analytical Psychology," on the other hand, recommended it. He claimed that not having a belief in life after death was a cause of neurosis. According to him any belief would do. One man thought people could be helped by excluding religion, the other thought the answer was to combine and distill truths from all religions.

Another major theorist of the 20th century, one who attended Union Theological Seminary and first set out to become a minister before becoming a psychologist, is Dr. Carl Rogers, founder of "Person Centered Psychology." His approach emphasizes the therapeutic (healing) value of what he gave the label “unconditional positive regard and empathy.”

This is clearly a re-wording and application of certain attributes of God's love (Jer. 31:34, Jn. 3:16 & 17, Ro. 5:8, Matt. 9:13, Heb. 5:1 - 2, & 8, I Jn. 4:10 & 19). However, his concept of a "non-directive" therapy has thrown the door wide open for all sorts of excesses. A vacuum of values simply does not exist. This concept became directive - toward immorality.

Seminaries, monasteries, and convents have long practiced "non-directive" counsel for novices who had to hear and decide for themselves what direction God was leading them in. At some point discipleship requires it. This has always been within the context of Christian values, something Rogers neglected to affirm. Much of the foundation for secular counseling is laid by co-opting truths found in the Christian faith.

The followers of Dr. Alfred Adler, a secular theorist who developed "Individual Psychology," would consider the Christian virtues of faith, hope, and love as necessary but not sufficient conditions of effective therapy. The willingness to take risks, or courage, is required to overcome neurotic self-defensiveness. The therapist is an encourager (faith builder?). For Adler, social interest is the highest goal. The great commandment Christ mention, “to love your neighbor as yourself," is the definition of mental health. **Leaving out the first commandment, loving God, is what most often separates humanist psychology from Biblical counseling** (Matt. 22:37-40).

Further connection can be found by considering the training of “Christian” counselors. The purpose of Clinical Pastoral Education (CPE) is to gain a working experience with special populations and combine the behavioral sciences with Theology. This training is one of the requirements for becoming a government minister such as a military chaplain. The authors of many counseling books written by and for Christians (such as myself) have both a degree from a religious school or seminary and from a secular school of psychology or counseling. Few Christian schools exist which specialize in counseling. Those that do are often staffed by professors with dual credentials.

Dr. Larry Crabb taught counseling at an evangelical school, Grace Theological Seminary in Indiana. His book Inside Out (1988), looks at what he calls "demandingness." This is a concept that was brought out earlier by the secular therapist, Dr. Albert Ellis, founder of "Rational-Emotive Therapy." It is commonly called lust, envy, greed, covetousness, or self-centeredness in the Bible (I Jn. 2:16, & Ja. 4:2 & 3). Dr. David Benner, a professor from still another evangelical school, Wheaton college in Illinois, wrote Healing Emotional Wounds, (1990). This explores learned, maladaptive responses to early trauma. This is a psycho-dynamic approach similar to "Cognitive Therapy," a secular system developed by Dr. Aaron Beck. The seeds of this can be found in the Bible too (Pro. 22:6, Col. 3:21).

The concept; "co-dependency," is a theoretical framework used by Christian counselors. It is used in the book Toxic Faith by Aterburn and Felton (1991) which explores how to heal damage that has been caused by religious excesses. This psycho-dynamic analysis grew out of studies of alcoholism. It is also used in the work of Minrith & Meier (1990) who apply it to many areas, including eating disorders and marriage relations.

Co-dependency is an intense emotional need (often due to the lack, as a child, of; love, attention, or nurturing), which a person attempts to fill by a fanatical adherence to something which is an inappropriate method or substitute. The person who is co-dependent will make excessive and unrealistic demands on the individual, group, or object which pretends to fulfill the need, or even partially satisfies it. The need is so great that much dysfunctional behavior will be allowed, or even actively supported, in order to maintain the familiar structure. There is a feeling or conviction that this lifestyle is normal or superior, and that any other or greater satisfaction would be impossible to find.

The co-dependence model is used to describe and explain adherence to cults among other things. It is altogether different from a spiritual hunger, or the need for God, though some may confuse the two desires. The healthy opposite of co-dependency is not mere independence but rather inter-dependency.

This analysis is another way of looking at the behavior which could be clinically labeled Borderline, Dependent, or Narcissistic Personality Disorder. Cult leaders such as Jim Jones or David Koresh or people in hate groups would be labeled as having Paranoid and/or Narcissistic Personality Disorder. They attract people with Dependant or Borderline Personality Disorders as followers.

Dr. Rollo May, an existential therapist points out two other neurotic conditions which may be called toxic faith. These are: an irrational sense of being invulnerable and an irrational belief in a personal protector, a servant/slave, at the beck and call of the believer. This manifests as a life spent searching for and appeasing a dominant "other," which leads to passivity, dependency and clinical depression. A more rational sense of eternal life and the protection of God acknowledges physical death, and accepts personal responsibility.

The promises and practices of many current "prosperity" or "hyper-faith" preachers could be called toxic faith. They use the same techniques described by Dr. Albert Ellis in his Rational-Emotive Therapy and Dr. Aaron Beck's Cognitive Therapy. These might be called applications of the Biblical admonition for the renewing of the mind (Ro. 12:2), or putting on the mind of Christ, but might better be described as brainwashing.

The process, in preaching or counseling, is to repeatedly castigate and rebuke followers for having any doubts, or worries, or lack of faith, about God's provision or blessing for them. This covers health, wealth, happiness or success. They have to replace all underlying doubts, or negative thoughts, with "faith," (and give money) then all will be well.

Dr. Beck proposed a more formal list of underlying maladaptive thoughts. He describes the extreme, of self-condemning, "shouldistic," thinking found in a maladjusted person's thought life. He believed each person maintains these thoughts through "self-talk" and mental images. These have to be changed for the client to change (Ja. 3:8). This is the new gospel of many evangelists and pastors who call it negative confession or doubt.

* * * * * * * *

A Christian counselor may develop his or her understanding of human personality from one source; the Bible, without considering individuals or people. Secular theorists may develop their theories from working with one group of disturbed individuals. One example of this is Dr. William Glasser. He worked with juvenile delinquents sentenced to detention centers. He developed "Reality Therapy" based on the observation that his clients had a poor self-image. He theorized from them, that people are what they perceive themselves to be; they have either a success identity (Phil. 4:13) or a failure identity.

These perceptions are developed early in life. However, Glasser discounts a client's history because he believes a person's self-image can be changed in the present without dealing with their past. This is similar to the concepts of Dr. Norman Vincent Peale, a minister, in his books <u>The Power of Positive Thinking</u> (1952), and <u>Dynamic Imaging</u> (1981). Healing methods that do not require digging up the past are popular with Christian and secular theorists.

There are multitudes of books and seminars on self-image, self-esteem, self-perception, self-concept, or self-worth (Pro. 23:7, Matt. 10:29-31). The Bible teaches that we were made in the image of God (Gen.1:26-27). This was broken by the fall and marred. It is the image of God, not the image of self, that needs to be restored (Ro. 8:29, II Cor. 3:18). There may need to be some clearing away of the fallen, and casting down, or out, before that can occur.

Dr. Jay Adams (1986), creator of his own "Christian Counseling" system, holds to concepts of mental health similar to Ellis and Beck: that we are what we think, and that we "self-indoctrinate," or sustain our own beliefs whether healthy or not. **The task of the counselor is to discover what these faulty messages are and get the client to recognize and change them** (II Cor. 10:5 & Phil. 4:8). Just adding "right" thoughts is like sowing seeds on hard ground (Jer. 4:3, Matt. 13:3-9).

Similarities between some Christian and secular theories can be seen in the "new" field of marriage and family counseling. A "systems" approach began to be used in the 1950s. In this the therapist worked with an entire family to see how it functioned as a system. Prior to this it was usually just one person in a family who had “the” problem who would be seen by any one therapist. The work of Virginia Satir, author of Conjoint Family Therapy (3rd ed. 1982), and Salvado Minuchin, founder of "Structural Therapy," are two examples.

Virginia Satir noticed a pattern repeated in many families. Two people each with low self-esteem, high expectations, and lack of trust get married to each other. They expect to receive something out of that marriage without a full awareness of how or what they need to give into it (Eph. 5:22 & 25). Their worst fears are realized when they discover there are differences between them. Next, each one labels differences "badness." More disagreements follow which get labeled a "lack of love."

Either partner then may attempt to satisfy their need for self-esteem through work, religion, or by parenting. That may result in what is called "triangulation;" an unbalanced relationship of one spouse with a child, in opposition to the other spouse. When either parent only gets emotional satisfaction by way of an intense relationship with a child it can be called emotional incest.

Many families live this way without being aware of it. They fail to learn: to accommodate differences, to trust, to build up each other's self-esteem, how to change false or unhelpful labels, or how to develop realistic expectations. The therapist attempts to teach these things. Satir also emphasizes the need to eliminate blaming and foster self-responsibility.

Minuchin described the kinds of structures and interactions found in a healthy family that are lacking in a dysfunctional family. The "spouse subsystem" is built by adjustment and negotiation of roles, with a balancing of contributions from each toward the essential needs of the marriage. Lists of "essential needs" may vary. Separate from this, is a "parental subsystem." It provides balance between firmness and nurturing, and clearly gives children the message that the parents are in charge, and authority is unequal. The "sibling subsystem" prepares the way for other peer relationships.

A healthy family will have clear, firm, yet flexible boundaries which delineate the amount and kind of contact allowed between individuals and subsystems. Boundaries that are too rigid indicate isolation and self-absorption resulting in inattention to the needs of others. Boundaries that are diffuse allow too much involvement in each other's business to the point of loss of independence and difficulty in recognizing one's own feelings. **Correcting faulty boundaries or interactions is the goal of therapy.**

There are similarities between secular and Christian therapeutic communities. Some examples are Synanon, for drug addicts, founded by Charles Dederick, and Teen Challenge, begun by David Wilkerson, both started in 1958. Youth For Christ group homes, foster care, and sanctuary, or "safe" houses are examples of community living centers which, like monasteries, have long been part of the teaching and healing regimen of the church.

* * * * * * * * *

It helps to use an "ecological" perspective of the client when trying to find faulty messages, patterns, boundaries or interactions. This includes: biology, sociology, anthropology, psychology, philosophy, and theology. Using scientific labels make this sound complicated or difficult. but it is simply their "context."

A counselor should consider the person's: physical state of health (biology). (Are they sober?) the social interactions and support systems (family, church, job, and community), how these compare with others (inner city poverty versus suburban middle class), the thinking and emotional state, (level, content, and stability), the view of the world, and the view of God. This could be called a psycho-social-biological-spiritual assessment. We do this all the time, only without those labels, or with different labels. Christianity aims at change at the most profound levels of the human soul which could, but does not always, effect all these areas.

Some counseling systems will use allegory, metaphor, symbolism and/or create rituals. Like other cognitive practices they attempt to replace abnormal thought structures and behaviors with healthy ones, or instill them for the first time. When the symbols are "Biblical" the system is called "Christian." Often however, there is just a thin veneer of spiritual language sprinkled in with what is basically a secular psychological approach. These approaches can be effective. They create confidence in the therapist.

This can be seen as a way of using the language people are most comfortable with or creating a new language they can easily use. When such a program reflects real needs and conditions it can be helpful. One old preacher remarked; "if you see a fellow riding into town on a camel, don't shoot the camel until you give him a horse." It may never be appropriate to "shoot someone's camel." However, the Bible is really a straight forward account of historical and spiritual facts. It does contain some allegory and symbolism. This should not be used as an excuse to obscure those healthy attitudes and relationships that were clearly spelled out in it long before psychology picked up on them. To mystify that which is clear, as some systems do, or to claim to create a brand new "Christian Psychology," does damage to the credibility of the Bible and to reality. We do this, in part, due to the historical and ongoing differences and hostility between the secular and Christian views.

"The fall of man" has been called a type or metaphor of abuse or abandonment. The "knowledge of good and evil" is thus a type of a maladaptive means of self-defense. The pride of "being like god," is a type of a neurotic, or false, sense of, or need for, security. Counseling thus becomes a substitute for conversion. This offers salvation from neurosis, or relief and freedom from real or imagined fear. This is not freedom from sin, reunion with God, and a new nature. Determining what the problem is that needs fixing and how to fix it is a problem.

There may be a "neurotic conversion experience" rather than a real encounter with God. It does not last. This is a counterfeit but it may serve a real need. Both may take place, not either/or. All have sinned but many are damaged further. The only real psychosis may be our being out of touch with the reality of God.

The charge is often leveled that psychology is prescribing moral anarchy when it calls certain thought patterns maladaptive or irrational ways of thinking rather than sin. The issue may be centered around the question of whether or not a person could apply his or her will-power and self-control. People with schizophrenia or Alzheimer's disease may not be considered responsible for their thoughts and actions. Those who willingly ingest substances that may cause them to lose control are considered responsible both legally and morally. Sick or Sinner is the question.

It gets even more confusing when we try to account for all the damaging and cruel experiences in life. Some people try to describe everything in terms of genetics, or as an "addiction," rather than as a choice. This is not unlike the question the disciples asked Jesus in regard to a man born blind ("who did sin?" (Jn. 9:2)). His response was to glorify God. Regardless of cause, or who should be responsible, the consequences can be severe. It has been estimated that the largest mental health institution in America is the Los Angeles County jail. Many states no longer allow an "insanity defense." Jail time is usually shorter without it.

The question can also be raised: "is the church preaching moral make-believe when it does not address the discrepancy between practice and belief?" Is the goal of being forgiven, and born again into an abundant life, to satisfy our lusts and natural needs, or is it to enliven and grow our spirits for an eternal existence? The Bible admonishes believers to examine themselves and it points out mankind's penchant for self-deception (Pro. 14:12, II Cor. 13:5). When a person recites the sinner's prayer and asks the Lord to come into his or her heart that person is not saved until and unless the Lord actually does come in. There is usually evidence of a transformed life, a new heart, and a new direction. Psychology and Christianity should not promote making excuses or make-believe or self produced faith.

There are those in both camps who hold to the concept that feelings of guilt, anger, shame, and fear are unhealthy. At times and for certain people these can be excessive, but they are a God-given, and healthy, part of our make-up. Much attention has been focused on the damage done by "false guilt," (also called "survivor's guilt"). This is the process of bearing shame or responsibility for something which the person had no control over. It is found in children who blame themselves for the divorce of their parents. It may also occur in the survivors of an accident where there were fatalities. This has led some people to a rejection of all guilt, or a rejection of standards that seem to create or allow for quilt and shame. This is an extreme gross misapplication. No counselor can avoid informing a client of the real consequences of their life style: AIDS, Herpes, the killing of an unborn child, heart disease, and cancer may not sound as final as Hell but the wages of sin is still death (Ro. 6:23).

* * * * * * * *

The connections and overlap described in this chapter cause some to bemoan The Psychological Seduction of Christianity (Babgan & Babgan 1987). The embracing of dream analysis, witchcraft, and even Eastern Religions in "Analytical Psychology," espoused by Dr. Carl Jung, is the sort of thing that, when occurring in churches or Christian counseling, might easily be labeled The Seduction of Christianity (Hunt, 1985). Nonetheless there is overlap, some of it valid and even useful.

A Christian counselor might rather work "...not in the words that man's wisdom teacheth, but which the Holy Ghost teacheth; comparing spiritual things with spiritual" (I Cor. 2:13). Unfortunately, we too often just assume we are spiritual. It is easy to make claims of power, when it is possible to avoid going to places where people have extreme needs. We may have much less power, discernment, common sense, or compassion than we like to think (I Cor. 3:1). At one time surgery and blood transfusions were looked upon as sacrilegious. Therapy has a similar bad reputation. However, for many people, teaching, or their ability to learn, is insufficient or their situation may be extremely abnormal. One useful definition of counseling is: **"a learning situation directed at those who have special problems or require special attention and techniques"** (I Cor. 15:46).

The intelligence God gave man works quite well to describe and name the world we live in. This includes ourselves and each other (Gen. 2:19). The fact that counselors from both Christian and secular backgrounds can see and describe the same mechanisms and types of personality development lends credence, not doubt, to the value of their analysis. We also do need to be aware of those who bring a perverse or unacceptable element into the process because we often do not clearly see our own hearts (Pro. 3:5 & 6, 12:15, & 21:2). And neither camp has endless resources nor absolute power.

The theories mentioned in this section do not necessarily exclude Biblical models of: **1) conviction, 2) confession, 3) repentance, 4) forgiveness, and 5) restitution**. They may help focus on ways certain areas of that pattern are blocked. Secular counselors have been slow to acknowledge the effect of gratitude on mental health, especially a grateful heart toward God. Some psychologists do however, realize the value of forgiveness and humility (Matt. 18:1-4, 15-17, 21-35, II Cor. 12:10, Ja. 4:6 & 10, I Pet. 5:5).

Psychology has turned forgiveness into self-help for the person who forgives, rather than a process of reconciliation. Many people need help learning how to apologize. They may start off trying to justify or explain an offense or say something like: "**if** I have in some way offended you," or they may address God or the therapist instead of the person they are trying to apologize to. An apology needs to clearly say "I was wrong, I know it and I am sorry, please forgive me." It may include the idea of trying not to do the same thing in the future and making amends or restitution. This sounds simple but may require a lot of re-learning.

* * * * * * * * *

The theories of the secular therapists: Freud, Jung, Adler, Rogers, Ellis, Beck, May, Glasser, Satir, and Minuchin are described in great detail in most counseling textbooks. Their own religious or spiritual state is not usually mentioned. They may be Jewish, Christian, Buddhist, atheist, or "other."

"Christian" counselors are those who believe in and acknowledge Jesus Christ as their Lord, God, and Savior, and supreme in their life, work, and affection. They may or may not practice a separate "Christian Psychology." Any explanation or theory of man that ignores God and the spiritual is incomplete, and may be false, or simply be bad science.

Chapter VIII Review

Pointing out the similarities and differences in theories is easier than actually counseling or working with people with difficult problems. Like a Monday morning armchair quarterback it is possible to make all the plays and get all the calls right. "Our side" comes out ahead and the "other side" loses. That sort of self-justification is not very helpful.

The purpose of this chapter is to help pastors recognize the kinds of treatment a client may have gone through, and what approaches are being used, regardless of whether they carry the label "Spiritual," or "Biblical," or "Christian psychology," or "secular psychology." If a counselor has only one way of viewing people, or just one method of counseling it may not matter. On the other hand, this may serve to highlight the value and strength of that one approach. Theories and systems are less important than the personality and strengths of the individual counselor. The theory or system he or she uses may only be a vehicle of convenience.

(Scripture references for Chapter VIII)

pg. 109 - Jer. 17:9 - The heart [is] deceitful above all [things], and desperately wicked: who can know it?

pg. 112 - Eph. 4:14 - That we [henceforth] be no more children, tossed to and fro, and carried about with every wind of doctrine, by the sleight of men...

pg. 113 - Jer. 31:34 - ...from the least of them unto the greatest of them, saith the LORD: ... I will forgive their iniquity, and I will remember their sin no more.

Jn. 3:16-17 - For God so loved the world, that he gave his only begotten Son, that whosoever believeth in him should not perish, but have everlasting life. **(17)** For God sent not his Son into the world to condemn the world; but that the world through him might be saved.

Ro. 5:8b - while we were yet sinners, Christ died for us.

Matt. 9:13 - But go ye and learn what [that] meaneth, I will have mercy, and not sacrifice: for I am not come to call the righteous, but sinners to repentance.

Heb. 5:1-2, 8 - For every high priest taken from among men is ordained for men in things [pertaining] to God, that he may offer both gifts and sacrifices for sins: **(2)** Who can have compassion on the ignorant, and on them that are out of the way; for that he himself also is compassed with infirmity. **(8)** Though he were a Son, yet learned he obedience by the things which he suffered;

1 Jn. 4:10, 19 - Herein is love, not that we loved God, but that he loved us, and sent his Son... for our sins. **(19)** We love him, because he first loved us.

Matt. 22:37 - 40 - Jesus said unto him, Thou shalt love the Lord thy God with all thy heart, and with all thy soul, and with all thy mind.**(38)** This is the first and the great commandment. **(39)** And the second is like unto it, Thou shalt love thy neighbor as thyself. **(40)** On these two commandments hang all the law and the prophets.

pg. 114 - I Jn. 2:16 - For all that [is] in the world, the lust of the flesh, and the lust of the eyes, and the pride of life, is not of the Father, but is of the world.

Ja. 4:2-3 - Ye lust, and have not: ye kill, and desire to have, and cannot obtain: ye fight and war, yet ye have not, because ye ask not. **(3)** Ye ask, and receive not, because ye ask amiss, that ye may consume [it] upon your lusts.

Pro. 22:6 - Train up a child in the way he should go: and when he is old, he will not depart from it.

Col. 3:21 - Fathers, provoke not your children [to anger]. lest they be discouraged.

pg. 116 - Ro. 12:2 - And be not conformed to this world: but be ye transformed by the renewing of your mind, that ye may prove what [is] that good, and acceptable, and perfect, will of God.

pg. 117 - Ja. 3:8 - But the tongue can no man tame; [it is] an unruly evil, full of deadly poison.

Phil. 4:13 - I can do all things through Christ which strengtheneth me.

pg. 118
Pro. 23:7 - For as he thinketh in his heart, so [is] he:....

Matt. 10:29-31 - Are not two sparrows sold for a farthing? and one of them shall not fall... without your Father. **(30)** But the very hairs of your head are all numbered. **(31)** Fear ye not therefore, ye are of more value than many sparrows.

Gen. 1:26-27 - And God said, Let us make man in our image, after our likeness... **(27)** So God created man in his [own] image, in the image of God created he him; male and female created he them.

Ro. 8:29 - For whom he did foreknow, he also did predestinate [to be] conformed to the image of his Son, that he might be the firstborn among many brethren.

II Cor. 3:18 - But we all, with open face beholding as in a glass the glory of the Lord, are changed into the same image from glory to glory, [even] as by the Spirit of the Lord.

II Cor. 10:5 - Casting down imaginations, and every high thing that exalteth itself against... God, and bringing into captivity every thought to the obedience of Christ;

Phil. 4:8 - ...whatsoever things are true, ...honest ...just ...pure ... lovely ...of good report; if [there be] any virtue, and ...any praise, think on these things.

Jer. 4:3 - For thus saith the LORD... Break up your fallow ground, and sow not among thorns.

Matt. 13:3-9 - ...a sower went forth to sow; **(4)** And when he sowed, some [seeds] fell by the way side, and the fowls came and devoured them up: **(5)** Some fell upon stony places...they had no deepness of earth: **(6)** And when the sun was up, they were scorched... they withered away. **(7)** And some fell among thorns; and the thorns... choked them: **(8)** But other fell into good ground, and brought forth fruit, some an hundredfold, some sixtyfold, some thirtyfold. **(9)** Who hath ears to hear, let him hear.

pg. 119
Eph. 5::22 & 25 - Wives, submit yourselves unto your own husbands, as unto the Lord. **(25)** Husbands, love your wives... as Christ also loved the church, and gave himself for it.

pg. 124
Jn. 9:2 - ...who did sin, this man or his parents, that he was born blind?

Pro. 14:12 - There is a way which seemeth right unto a man, but the end thereof [are] the ways of death.

II Cor. 13:5 - Examine yourselves, whether ye be in the faith; prove your own selves.

pg. 125
Ro. 6:23 - For the wages of sin [is] death; but the gift of God [is] eternal life through Jesus Christ our Lord.

pg. 126
Gen. 2:19 - ...the LORD God formed every beast of the field, and every fowl of the air; and brought [them] unto Adam to see what he would call them: and whatsoever Adam called every living creature, that [was] the name...

Pro. 3:5 & 6 - Trust in the LORD with all thine heart; and lean not unto thine own understanding. **(6)** In all thy ways acknowledge him, and he shall direct thy paths.

Pro. 12:15 - The way of a fool [is] right in his own eyes: but he that hearkeneth unto counsel [is] wise.

Pro. 21:2 - Every way of a man [is] right in his own eyes: but the LORD pondereth the hearts.

I Cor. 2:13, 3:1, - Which things also we speak, not in the words which man's wisdom teacheth, but which the Holy Ghost teacheth; comparing spiritual things with spiritual. **(3:1)** And I..., could not speak unto you as unto spiritual, but as unto carnal, [even] as unto babes in Christ.

I Cor. 15:46 - ...that [was] not first which is spiritual, but that which is natural; and afterward that which is spiritual.

pg. 127
Matt. 18:1-4, 15-17, ...Who is the greatest in the kingdom of heaven? **(2)** And Jesus called a little child unto him... **(3)** And said... Except ye be converted, and become as little children, ye shall not enter into the kingdom of heaven. **(4)** Whosoever therefore shall humble himself as this little child, the same is greatest in the kingdom of heaven. **(15)** Moreover if thy brother shall trespass against thee, go and tell him his fault between thee and him alone: if he shall hear thee, thou hast gained thy brother. **(16)** But if he will not hear [thee, then] take with thee one or two more, that in the mouth of two or three witnesses every word may be established. **(17)** And if he shall neglect to hear them, tell [it] unto the church: but if he neglect to hear the church, let him be unto thee as an heathen man and a publican.

Matt 18: 21-35 - Then came Peter to him, and said, Lord, how oft shall my brother sin against me, and I forgive him? till seven times? **(22)** Jesus saith unto him, I say not unto thee, Until seven times: but, Until seventy times seven. **(23)** Therefore is the kingdom of heaven likened unto a certain king, which would take account of his servants. **(24)** ... one was brought unto him, which owed him ten thousand talents. **(25)** But... he had not to pay, his lord commanded him to be sold,... **(26)** The servant therefore fell down... saying, Lord, have patience with me, and I will pay thee all.

(27) Then the lord ...was moved with compassion, and loosed him, and forgave him the debt. **(28)** But the same servant... found one of his fellowservants, which owed him an hundred pence: and he laid hands on him, and took [him] by the throat, saying, Pay me that thou owest. **(29)** And his fellowservant fell down at his feet... saying, Have patience with me, and I will pay thee all. **(30)** And he would not:... **(31)** So when his fellowservants saw what was done, they ...came and told unto their lord all... **(32)** Then his lord ...said unto him, O thou wicked servant, I forgave thee all that debt ... **(33)** Shouldest not thou also have had compassion on thy fellowservant, even as I had pity on thee? **(34)** And his lord... delivered him to the tormentors,... **(35)** So likewise shall my heavenly Father do also unto you, if ye from your hearts forgive not every one his brother...

II Cor. 12:10 - ...I take pleasure in infirmities, in reproaches, in necessities, in persecutions, in distresses for Christ's sake: for when I am weak, then am I strong.

Ja. 4:6 & 10 - But he giveth more grace... God resisteth the proud, but giveth grace unto the humble. **(10)** Humble yourselves in the sight of the Lord, and he shall lift you up.

I Pet. 5:5 - ...be subject on to another ...with humility...

How can theory just be convenience? Dr. Karl Jung discovered that many of his rich clients were drug or alcohol abusers. He listened to them for an hour or two until they finally admitted the problem.

IX - Techniques

"Strengthen ye the weak hands and confirm the feeble knees" (Is. 35:3).

It has been said that when the only tool you have is a hammer, everything begins to look like a nail. This chapter will first look at some secular techniques in counseling. The scriptural roots of these will be noted when they are easily inferred. Some means that are specific to Christianity will also be mentioned. After this some techniques that appear to be common to both will be noted.

There is a rush for the latest "fad of the month." Today the hottest thing in counseling is recovering memories and dreams, which is as old as Joesph or the book of Daniel. The present form relies on help from hypnosis, drugs, or trances and not, as Daniel claimed, only God. Another current craze is Multiple Personality Disorder which became popular after books and movies here publicized it.

Radio and TV talk shows attract audiences with testimonies of cruelty, and extreme suffering, and the suggestion that there are techniques and experts who can repair any damage. There are not. The things included in this chapter will not be familiar to everyone but the attempt has been made to avoid any single-minded or extreme approach.

The therapeutic relationship, all by itself, may be the most important element of change. It may be labeled therapy, teaching, re-parenting, mentoring, or pastoring, discipling, spiritual directing, modeling, or advising, guidance, peer counseling or friendship (II Tim. 2:24 & 25). To be a healthy relationship it should grow out of the interaction of two or more real people and not out of some mystical or pseudo-scientific jargon or mythical illusions: a collar or a tie, a steeple, a confessional, an office wall with diplomas, or a new growth group. Demystification does not remove that which is real and valuable. Respect for a person requires being open and honest.

The therapist's personality is as important as the practice. Counselors need to have reached a level of self-awareness and to have dealt with their own conflicts enough so as to be moving toward a greater degree of mental health themselves. Training or a book can only enhance what is already there. They cannot make a person into a counselor.

It has been estimated that 80% of all pastors and counselors have experienced serious problems themselves. Resolving or simply enduring these is often the motivation for becoming a counselor or a pastor. However, two people facing the same condition may view it in different ways. **Keep in mind that what worked in one case will not necessarily work for someone else.**

We need to have an understanding of a "healthy personality" not just pathology or what it means to be sick, or how to fix someone. This gives a standard to compare with and an idea of what direction to aim for. The Bible, and a healthy Christian community, should be the primary source for this. The "modern" view measures mental health by work and love. The goal is being stable on the job and in a family.

Raymond Corsini (1991) points out common practices among counselors. Comparing these to scripture can demonstrate how old these insights are. The techniques used to convey a message or produce an effect may differ. They can even sometimes contradict. None-the-less there are many obvious similarities. These reflect a common understanding of what "normal" or healthy and human means.

Some factors are: universalization - realizing you are not the only one with the problem and that you are not alone (I Cor. 10:13), insight - self-understanding and perspective (Pro. 20:27, 21:2, II Cor. 13:5), and thirdly, modeling - by the therapist or others (I Cor. 11:1, Heb. 12:2). In addition there is: acceptance - being part of a group and receiving unconditional positive regard (Eph. 1:6&7), altruism - being loved and giving love or care (Jn. 15:12-15, Gal. 6:10, I Jn. 4:19-21), and connectedness - the emotional bond with the therapist or group members (Ro. 12:10, I Cor. 4:15, Eph. 2:19).

Counseling also includes: reality testing; such as learning and trying out of new behaviors, including opportunities to be productive (II Cor. 5:7, Phil. 4:13). There is a need for expression - shouting, crying, expressing anger and still being accepted (Acts 15:39, II Tim. 4:11, Eph 4:26), and interaction - open discussion and confession (Jas. 5:16). This list of mechanisms of counseling could be a description of good mental health in a healthy individual, family, church, or community.

Things that promote the opposite tendencies are unhealthy. A lack of love, extreme self-denial or self-centeredness are obvious examples. Those things that promote exclusivity, secretiveness, or isolationism may also be harmful.

The first mechanism, just knowing that others have problems too and you are not the only one in your particular situation, can be a source of hope. It can be viewed as an application of the scripture; "There hath no temptation taken you but such as is common to man: but God is faithful, who will not suffer you to be tempted above that you are able; but will with the temptation also make a way to escape, that ye may be able to bear it." (I Cor. 10:13). Some interpret that scripture to mean that God will remove the problem before it becomes unbearable. What it says is that He will give us the strength or show us a way to bear it.

Reality testing should allow the client to see inconsistencies and contradictions. Situations can be set up to test assumptions, instead of arguing over reality. A counselor may empower other people in relationship with the client, or sabotage the client's systems, in order to cause change.

* * * * * * * * *

Counseling has often been called **"detective work." It can be seen as a search for the cause of a problem or for what is preventing a person from solving their own problems**. Counselors mainly talk, ask questions, and help clients talk and give expression to their thoughts and feelings. They may help a person endure suffering, grieve loss, or express anger. They listen, observe, model healthy behavior and relationships, give directions for tasks, or arrange for an experience or a setting, to help resolve present, past, or future problems.

* * * * * * * * *

Counselors may be **teachers and/or doers** who **create** a corrective experience to try to compensate for a lack in development. It can be appropriate to **help** a client find a job. <u>The Very Quick Job Search</u> (Farr, 1990), is a good resource to have on hand to help when doing vocational counseling. Someone might need a place to live or need to get in contact with other appropriate service providers. The goal is to teach clients how to go about doing these things on their own but that goal may take awhile to reach.

Secular counselors may teach Christian morality but call it "adult logic." Some examples are: The Golden Rule (Matt. 7:12), forgiveness (Lk. 6:37), or peace (Ro. 12:18-19). Specific skills training such as: relaxation training, budgeting, or generating and writing out a problem list, can help get counseling started and organized. Note taking and record keeping are vital for most practices. A written contract may be helpful for a marriage. When resistance to change is a problem it can help to negotiate a financial contract using bargaining, and setting prices, and writing them down.

* * * * * * * *

Accurate **rephrasing** and **clarifying** can help the client give expression, or names, to feelings. As past memories, or more recent experiences, are explored the therapist may **define** and **label** them or even suggest appropriate responses. Parents do this for children, teachers do it for students, and pastors do it for their congregations (Ecc. 3:1&4). Emotional counseling is aimed at helping a person explore their feelings verbally by connecting them to thoughts. A child, or an adult, may have been unable to respond, or been overwhelmed by an event or trauma. These may have been repressed or misinterpreted. He or she may need to explore and experience painful emotions in a safe, appropriate manner. Keeping painful or unacceptable emotions and memories repressed requires a great deal of emotional energy.

The release of this, called catharsis, frees the person's full potential and avoids uncontrolled release in thoughts, dreams, actions, or physical illnesses (Heb. 12:15, Jas. 3:14, Ps. 19:12). The purpose is to empower the person to handle the present problem by resolving distracting roots. The release may be of repressed emotions; stored "bad feelings" that were never expressed. It does not have to be a recall of traumatic events. There may just be a release of accumulated tension and stress.

There are three problems with memory work. First, without a means of dealing with the "unfinished business" the result may be a freedom to become a self-righteous, angry, victim. Second memories may be fabricated for a client by a counselor who is working through his or her own grief. Related to this, thirdly, there may not be a reliable way to validate content. Memories are not reliable as to factual content. None-the-less, many people report that the emotional release is helpful.

Christians may discover a depth or memory within them untouched by the love of Christ. They need to invite the Lord to enter "their inner most being" and deal with what is there. Inner Healing is careful to do this. This is part of the continuing process of sanctification. Many churches today are blessed with an outpouring of Spiritual "new wine" which seems to bring a healing emotional release.

A theory or a diagnosis of pathology or human development, whether it is true or false, accurate or not, should result in some precise ways to work, or not work with problems. Diagnosis is never complete without a plan of action. Otherwise it is just a label or bad name to hang on someone.

Neurotics have been defined as being overly concerned with their own protection or superiority. One approach, to change this unhealthy position, is to use role playing to get another point of view. A counselor could expose a person's intentions in such a way as to make them distasteful, perhaps by using exaggeration, or by wish fulfillment; that is asking the question "suppose you get everything you want," or "what if...," or "act as if...."

A variation on the "what if..." question is the miracle question. "Suppose you wake up tomorrow and during the night, while you slept, a miracle had taken place which solved this problem. What would be different? How would you be, and what would you do differently?" Another way of wording this is: "if you sent me a post card next year after your problems were past, what would have happened? What would you be doing?" A third way is to ask: "if this mountain were mole hill what would your life be like?" This gives a sense of hope by pointing to what could work. The goal is to find realistic answers to fulfill this, not simply: "I would win the Lottery."

This approach focuses on solutions that exist in a healthy environment - not on trying to find the cause and unravel the "why" of problems. **The therapist and client look for small steps to take to actually achieve, or live in, "the miracle."** This is called Brief Therapy. It was developed in the mid-1980's by Steve de Shazer (Phil. 4:8). It builds on a Rogerian point of view which sees clients as having their own resources and solutions for life's problems. A scripture to coincide with that is Luke 17:21 "...the kingdom of God is within you." The purpose of counseling is to help a person release it. Narrative therapy, the telling of positive self-stories, is another variation on this.

Other useful questions to ask are: "how have you coped with problems or feelings like this in your past?" "When were things better?" "What was going on then?" Answers should be elicited in terms of positive changes and behaviors rather than in feelings. Feelings should be acknowledged but the focus should be on: "what were you doing?"

Counselors can try to elicit solutions from clients rather than trying to fix or rescue them. In counseling, solutions being offered are often rebutted with a "yes but... ." These questions put the responsibility for change with the client. "Yeabutters" are re-directed to their experience. This is not a quick fix. It may not even be brief.

Clients can be helped to explore their self-concept and self-regard by use of card sorting. A character trait is written on each card and the client places them in order from first to last. The order may change weekly or daily. Another similar technique is scaling. Clients rate their situation today on a scale of 1 (bad) to 10 (great). Next they rate the problem tomorrow, then the focus is on finding variations. Is it worse than or better than: last week, or yesterday, <u>what is different</u>? <u>Why</u>? Teaching people to focus on their own behaviors helps to empower them to make their own changes. They keep track with a card sort or a self-scale and note why changes do or do not occur.

> Not everyone can learn to be self-aware. Motivation for this may be absent. It helps for the counselor to consider who is actually the client. If change is not desired, is resisted, or is contingent upon others, such as other family members, then solutions have to be found elsewhere.

Paradoxing or negative practice is a more complex technique. In this the counselor, instead of contradicting the client, becomes an ally, by exaggeration, or by agreeing with the maladaptive symptoms. This is done in order to force the client to expose faulty logic and refuse to continue with the behavior. This practice has been called using judo instead of boxing with a client (Prov. 26:5).

The therapist must observe patterns, not just specific symptoms, to try to discover the purpose the symptoms are trying to fulfill. By examining the environment a counselor may find out which problems are essential to work on or are even real. A major change in personality may not be needed if variations in external patterns or events can help create the desired change or resolve a problem.

For example; if a person's boundaries are too rigid or too diffuse, they employ either-or, all or nothing, black and white thinking, or blaming and absolute thinking, these may be the signs of stress or depression rather than symptoms of a borderline personality disorder. The depression needs to be alleviated and the thought disorders will disappear. Working only on the maladaptive thoughts will not produce change. These need to be brought to the client's attention at a later time so that he or she can become aware of the patterns resorted to when stress hits. Each of us can learn how to be our own therapist.

* * * * * * * *

Just teaching right from wrong is excellent counsel. After generations of broken homes many people have no idea how to live together in peace. Those who have not had healthy family role models need to be taught to simply talk about relationships (Jer. 4:22). People need to be taught to **self-reflect** and **self-monitor**.

A person may be unaware of how they avoid communication. There may be hidden techniques used to avoid intimacy. A client may need to learn ways in which to communicate better and resolve conflicts, such as negotiation and compromise.

* * * * * * * *

One estimate is that 85% of all the problems marriage counselors have presented to them have to do with money issues. These are not impossible to resolve. Divorce however, can be predicted with a very high degree of accuracy in couples whose patterns of communication have become marked by: 1) defensiveness, or by 2) denial, 3) or criticism, and 4) contempt, 5) sarcasm, and/or 6) physical, mental, or emotional withdrawal (Eph. 5:24 & 25, Jas. 5:9). Those couples which exhibit anger, and deal with it, are more likely to survive than those who shut off the expression of feelings or talking. Restricted patterns of communication and having too many secrets is destructive.

* * * * * * * *

One therapist put it as: "anything goes as long as it works." That may seem too open, but it is not meant to invite extremes. This can include: singing and dancing, playing or learning to play a musical instrument, working with clay, painting, humor (Pro. 17:22), or whatever the imagination can come up with as long as it is ethical, moral and the therapist and client are comfortable with it. There needs to be a mutual evaluation of the style and intent of the therapist and the client.

There is often a need to examine values. If either person is antagonistic to Christian values, or any others, it should be made known and a more appropriate match made. The counseling setting may be a time to work on **value clarification** but it is not an excuse to indoctrinate someone in the guise of "mental health." Lack of morals may be the root cause of a problem but an unsaved person may not be able to simply adopt Biblical Christian values. The therapist's values and prejudices need to be acknowledged as well as the client's.

* * * * * * * *

Psychological tests, such as a Minnesota Multi-Phasic Personality Inventory (MMPI), or Aaron Beck's Depression Inventory, are used for diagnostic purposes. They look for the existence of, and measure the severity of, a problem. The Self-Directed Survey (SDS), uses John Holland's theory to help people discover certain personality traits such as: realistic, conventional, enterprising, investigative, artistic, or social.

The Meyers-Briggs Inventory measures extroversion and introversion. It should be noted that the concept for the Meyers-Briggs Inventory was developed from Carl Jung's theories which he based on the Taoist teaching of "Yin and Yang." This is the belief in eternal, essential, inescapable, inter-twined, opposites in nature, such as good/evil, light/dark, male/female.

The Bible views free will and individual personality as sacred. It does not "require" evil as the other half of good. The Taoist or Buddhist view of the inter-relationship of all things is not a revelation from Christ. Another test, popular with some churches, uses "types" found in ancient Greek philosophy. The church's doctrines have been interwoven with Greek philosophy from its beginning. Just discovering what "type" a person is may help them adjust or help with a career search. Instead, it may only give a meaningless label and limit a person's choices.

Aptitude, achievement, personality or interest, tests can enhance a client's understanding. Tests can help evaluate the progress of therapy. Environmental inventories can give a picture of the functioning of a marriage, family, work, or school setting. Testing is a major component in school guidance counseling or vocational counseling to measure skill level. Tests have an almost mystical "scientific" aura about them. However, they are much less revealing than the general public believes. **Tests do not work by themselves. They can only give clues to suggest areas to look into more carefully but they are not by themselves valid.** The proper use, evaluation, and application of tests should be in the context of an over all counseling strategy and not just a one time "shot in the dark," or screening, which may only exclude, frighten, or titillate. Feedback and follow through after the test is a vital component of all testing.

Counselors will get more or less detailed background information on the client. Some family therapists gather the whole family in order to get several viewpoints. With everyone present the therapist will observe: styles of communication, interlocking relations, boundaries, and the roles being used. This helps when people have difficulty seeing themselves, or have "selective" memories.

The cost of counseling and insurance limits make efficient use of time essential. One time saving technique for diagnosis is the *geno-gram*. The client is asked to fill in a chart describing his or her family of origin. This is a simple form with boxes for males, circles for females, and triangles, with a B or S inside, for siblings. An *eco-map* (ecology-map) is added to the genetic chart. This answers specific questions. The client may be asked to draw arrows between people who were close and X's between those who did not get along well. Crisis or changes, such as divorce, or death, can be noted. After an initial interview charts can be designed to highlight things relevant to the particular counseling situation.

This technique can be used to quickly find out the condition of the grandparent's family or a present family. The present family is compared to the families of origin to see if patterns are being repeated. Different family members can each come up with an eco-map so the therapist can compare how each person's perspective of the family agree or differ.

Counseling includes just listening or actively "being there." Help can be given in the form of practicing tasks, or rehearsal, to prepare for an approaching problem. Rituals, drama, or dance, are other creative ways to help people gain insight and understanding. Audio or video tapes of counseling sessions, or of some specific situations, or specific reading assignments can help promote discussion or aid in diagnosis. Counselors explain, describe, and illustrate. They interpret, validate, dispute, persuade, and also challenge irrational beliefs. They coach, confirm, confide, comfort, and confront. The client may be taught how to accept reality, or responsibility, or to delay gratification. The distinction between wants and needs may need to be taught. A person may need to learn to give up deifying and vilifying, or to give up false absolutes such as "shoulds," "oughts," or magic.

* * * * * * * *

"The Serenity Prayer," of Reinhold Niebuhr, asks the Lord for help to change what can be changed, to be able to put up with what cannot be changed, and to know how to tell the difference between the two. This prayer was made popular by Alcoholics Anonymous. Their 12 step program is a model of Biblical discipleship. This approach has been used by groups working on any number of problems including; violence, lust, overeating, overspending, and gambling. The 12 steps can be applied to many needs with little or no change. The are easy to understand, but not so easy to apply.

The 12 steps of Alcoholics Anonymous are:

1) We admit to being powerless over alcohol (or whatever the problem is) and that our life has become unmanageable because of it.
2) We come to believe that a power greater than ourselves could return us to sanity.
3) We decide to turn our will and lives over to the love and care of God (as we understand him).
4) We make a searching and fearless inventory of ourselves.
5) We admit to God, ourselves, and another human being the exact nature of our wrongs.
6) We are ready to have God remove all these defects of character.
7) We humbly ask him to remove our short comings.
8) We make a list of all persons we have harmed and become willing to make amends to them all.
9) We make direct amends to such people whenever possible except when to do so would injure them or others.
10) We continue to make personal inventory and when we are wrong promptly admit it.
11) We seek through prayer and meditation to improve our conscious contact with God (as we understand him) praying only for knowledge of His will for us and the power to carry it out.
12) Having had a spiritual awakening as a result of these steps, we will try to carry this message to alcoholics (or whatever population this group is) and to practice these principles in all our affairs.

There are Christian AA groups for whom the God of their understanding is Jesus Christ. The 12 step program of AA is very much a pattern of Christian discipleship yet the group works to avoid being labeled "Christian." This is in part because many alcoholics (and others who use the 12 steps) had considered themselves Christian all their lives, even while they lived as drunks, gamblers, debtors or whatever. Instead of finding help in church they found empty ritual, or worse yet, condemnation. Another reason to avoid the label is to attract people form various backgrounds. These are also some of the reasons for the rise of independent "Christian Counselors." Real and serious problems were being ignored, glossed over, or spiritualized, or the people who had them were simply rejected.

* * * * * * * *

Pastors may focus only on spiritual growth. They may understand counseling to mean only a more personalized approach or attempt to interpret and apply scripture truths to a person's life. This can often be excellent counseling. On the other hand, some people have come to expect a rehash of last Sunday's sermon if they go to their pastor for counsel on Monday. Some counselors and pastors have just one model or mindset and find the same (or latest) problems or use the same approach with everyone they see. Some counselors have been accused of planting thoughts or problems in a client's mind according to their own pet theory. We are not perfect.

"Where is Christ in all this?" This should be the first question a Christian counselor asks. **"What does God want of me and of this other person?"** Looking to God first can save much time and wasted effort. **"How can he or she be led to the cross?"** These concerns or prayers need to be raised before other actions or techniques are used.

How can we get any truths or theories to work? Should we try to recreate a Garden of Eden without a commandment or the fruit? Should we just seek after miracles? Should we consistently and swiftly punish wrong, and reward right thoughts and behavior? A broad over-all spiritual training approach, <u>Discipleship</u>, which in many ways resembles counseling, is often used. This works with individuals, couples, families, or with small groups. There are other types of Christian counseling systems directed toward more specific problem solving. <u>Prayer Counseling</u> expands upon the basic model of expressing a need and then receiving prayer and perhaps advice. This may include a prescribed list of problems to look for and pray about. <u>Inner Healing</u> is similar to this but aims to deal with memories of past events. More time is allowed to explore the problem and the past and in particular the place of God in what has transpired. <u>Deliverance</u> is different from these methods in that the primary focus is on combating evil spiritual influence, oppression, or possession.

Since demonic power may work through the avenue of painful memories these four approaches sometimes overlap. These are thorough approaches which may work with any area of need. They try to combat all destructive influences but especially any spiritual ones. They may occur during or right after the church service or in special sessions.

Prayer and other **spiritual ministries** have the positive natural effect of allowing a person to share needs in a caring environment. However, they function most fully and effectively when the people involved actually have received Saving Grace, Spiritual Regeneration, and the Christian Graces which then become available. This empowering is usually not acquired by just talking about it, claiming or confessing it, however, there is a need to teach about, seek for, and remind ourselves of, spiritual reality lest we succumb to the pull of the earthly.

The **Holy Spirit** empowers understanding of the Bible and gives special **gifts** for ministry and counseling such as: a word of wisdom, or a word of knowledge, or the gift of prophecy, which is used to comfort, edify and to exhort. The gift of faith, gifts of healing, the discerning of spirits, the working of miracles, divers kinds of tongues, and interpretation of tongues are also available gifts (I Cor. 12: 4-11). These function at any time, not just during church services, or in or for counseling sessions.

Spiritual fruit is another major area of spiritual counsel (Gal. 5:22-23). These are often interpreted as referring to natural character. In this respect they help with living, in service, as models, and for instruction. More importantly, for effectual work in counseling or any ministry, those who allow the Lord to cultivate and grow spiritual fruit in their lives will have developed within them **spiritual substance** which can be imparted to others in need. This substance, or fruitfulness, unlike a gift, requires nurturing.

Someone who has been hurt or is greatly agitated needs to feed on the fruit of longsuffering, or on love, joy, and peace. Someone in need of a change in their personality or character may need to feed on the fruit of meekness, gentleness, or goodness. The fruit of faith or temperance can help someone struggling with self-control. These are just partial examples of spiritual transfusions.

This impartation often comes by personal prayer and laying on of hands. On the other hand, being spiritually hungry and *near* a fruitful person may be all it takes to partake of his or her spiritual substance. Intercessory prayer works without direct contact between the parties involved. A person in need of spiritual substance may receive it with or without any obvious physical contact. This can be discerned just as Jesus knew when virtue or power to heal was gone out from him (Mk. 5:30).

An openness in a person's spiritual life to receive gifts and grow and cultivate fruit may begin the preparation and anointing for **office ministries to the church** (Eph. 4:11-12, I Cor. 12: 28). Each of these offices has a particular emphasis or flavor in the way they counsel. An Apostle tends more toward essential beginnings, foundational or governmental expression. A Prophet or Seer may describe as well as deliver a divine message. An Evangelist will inspire and stir up. A Pastor will nurture and a Teacher instructs. Different individuals with the same office may have strengths in particular areas.

The ministry of the operations of gifts, fruit, and offices are not exclusive or unique. They can overlap, interact, function in other ways, not just in counseling, and to varying degrees. The gift or fruit of faith may bring assurance of the reality of God or may be more narrowly focused toward a specific need or event. A person in the office of a Pastor may function in a Prophetic way, or with Apostolic authority.

Every born-again child of God has **spiritual senses** which develop as we grow spiritually. Our spiritual senses allow us to: see, hear, smell, taste, touch, and discern movement or position in the spiritual realm. With these we can discern the manifest presence of God, the moving of the Holy Spirit, the operation of Spiritual gifts, the presence of Spiritual fruit, and recognize office ministries.

Spiritual ministries: gifts, fruit, offices, and senses are included in this chapter because they impart healing and counsel. This is not to imply that they are skills to employ nor to equate them with natural means (Acts 8:18-20). They originate from the anointing of God on a person's life. They are not learned techniques. **The Spirit of Counsel** (Is. 11:2) is greater than the sum of its parts.

Spiritual gifting or clinical expertise is no guarantee of counseling success. Some people just want to be listened to but not change. Fear, pride, stress, or a need to self-protect, or a desire to "get even," can block any effort. Without an ability to be led, some **meekness and humility**, a person may not be able to receive help (Matt. 11:28-30, Zeph. 2:3).

Many secular techniques resemble Christian practices. Both Christians and non-Christians can be helped by similar things. A common technique is specific task setting. These can be suggestions to do, or think about doing, something that would be pleasing to someone else (like good works?). Another technique is talking to an empty chair as though someone were sitting in it with whom you could not talk (like praying?). Another technique used is talking to a part of your own self that you need to deal with (self-examination?). Doing good works, or just talking to someone else, or yourself, out loud, can help a person feel better or gain some insight.

The client can be taught to create images of thoughts, actions, or values, such as touching a hot stove (like fear of hell?), as cues to **self-monitor** an unwanted behavior or a new one to be learned. The image of "changing channels" to go back and forth between emotional situations and states can prove that one has control over emotions and not the other way around (the view from eternity?). The therapist can help the client create an image or experience that is comforting or pleasant, such as the arms of a loving parent (likr God?), which gives a safe place to retreat to when things become too overwhelming. These are a normal part of church life but may be missing from the life of a non-churched person.

* * * * * * * *

There is a denial busting technique used by speakers at large church groups, or at conventions of national para-church groups, or in smaller church retreats. The speaker, who is a stranger, but has respect and stature as a mature individual, talks about or confesses having to struggle with impure thoughts, motives, or feelings, such as lust, envy, jealousy, pride, or anger. The listeners are encouraged that it is possible to be a Christian and still experience these things. They may be directed to form groups, then or later, where they can be honest with others and deal with their hidden feelings (I Jn. 1:8-10, Rev. 2:23). This is also used by secular speakers and groups to open discussion on any number of hidden things.

Music is often used in therapy to create an environment or to help establish rapport. It is useful for physical or emotional movement. The actual content of songs can be a powerful way to focus on issues, touch emotions, and help give expression to both good and bad feelings. Singing "the blues" or singing joyful songs has long been a helpful way of dealing with life (Job 35:10). Shakespeare wrote "music hath charms to soothe the savage breast." (I Sam 16:23). **Worship and praise are two powerful weapons of Spiritual warfare which release both natural and spiritual healing processes.**

* * * * * * * *

Music, and many other techniques used in grief counseling, may be helpful for anyone. Believers who have suffered a loss have the peace and the comfort of knowing we have a heavenly home. There is meaning and purpose to our lives and suffering, and *perhaps even the presence of God and His angels now*. Death is only a passage, a temporary separation for Christians, it is not annihilation or nonexistence. We can acknowledge it, and sorrow over a temporary loss. We may suffer, and feel pain, but we do not have to succumb to hopelessness (I Thes. 4:13 & 18).

The questions asked during a severe crisis such as "why?" can best be understood as being a way of saying: "I hurt, what can I do about it, or how can I adjust?" Those who try to help will grow from the experience. However, no-one is an "expert" with anyone else's situation. Mistakes that hurt can be made when trying to help someone in pain. Forgive yourself, and be more careful next time.

Here are some suggestions for dealing with grieving drawn from many sources that may help. To begin with: use the name of the person, or the name of the illness, or the usual name of the problem, not euphemistic expressions. Dead is dead, not "expired." Cancer is cancer, not "it." Do not try to exclude children from knowledge of a tragedy. Tell them what they need to know, want to know, and can understand, in a manner that is appropriate to their age. For young children use examples the child is familiar with. Each person, young or old, should be free to express how they feel and think. Do not force a certain response.

Loss can be a time of major life change and character building. Use it, seek after and look for this. You may not get all the answers, or resolve all the problems or pain, but the attempt can be beneficial. Search for meaning. A time of loss may become a time of discovery (Ro. 8:28). Earned understanding may sound like age-old, learned wisdom, but it belongs to each one of us in a special way.

There is no one right pattern to follow. How a person responds, or not, is his or her choice. Do not demand a specific grieving behavior or time. Do not try to handle or control feelings - feel them. Find ways to give expression to the loss. Give yourself and others the freedom to fall apart, or go "crazy." You will be safe, and get through it, with family and friends around, but especially if you fall into the arms of the Lord Jesus Christ.

A person's reactions to any loss may stem from and include reactions to other losses faced in life. The memory of other severe problems and the reaction to them may rise to the surface along with the current one. A grieving person may be trying to make sense of what has happened by talking. He or she may be thinking out loud, **not** asking for a reply. When, or if, you do respond, use your own feelings, not clichés. **Listen more and talk less.**

Trust people to lead you in your efforts to help. They may at times seem confused or angry, but they may also really know what it is they need. Try to be specific with any offers of help. Treat each person as a whole individual, not as if the problem or loss is all that there was to them. Allow the person some privacy. A major loss can take a long time to adjust to. Be involved over time and frequently pray for them. Loss effects us all, as John Dunn said: "ask not for whom the bell tolls, it tolls for me and thee."

Chapter IX Review

The professional techniques in this chapter are similar to scripture, and common sense, or something a parent, a grandparent, a teacher, or a pastor might say. A song in The Sound of Music, says "...when I'm feeling sad, I simply remember my favorite things, and then I don't feel so bad." That is good counsel! (Phil. 4:8). The problem with common sense is that it is not very common.

The Spiritual operations may seem or sound too incredible. One of the gifts of the Holy Spirit is the discernment of spirits (literally spirituals or spiritual things). Those who disclaim the gifts must also disclaim this one. How then can they discern anything as being spiritual, or natural, or non-existing, without the gift of discerning spiritual things? Honest scientists or theologians can only say that something is beyond their experience or beyond their ability to measure. They might also say they are not interested or do not want to be involved.

Both the natural and the spiritual means of counseling described in this chapter take place all the time for those who have the sort of support network of friends, family and church that provides these things. They may take place or be present in a preventative or a maintenance way, as well as during times of special need. Very often it is the people who are not plugged into a support network that require special counseling sessions or professional care.

(Scripture references for chapter IX)

pg. 135
Is. 35:3 - Strengthen ye the weak hands, and confirm the feeble knees.

pg.136 - II Tim. 2:24 & 25 - And the servant of the Lord must not strive; but be gentle unto all [men], apt to teach, patient, **(25)** In meekness instructing those that oppose themselves; if God... will give them repentance to the...truth;

pg.137
I Cor. 10:13 - There hath no temptation taken you but such as is common to man: but God is faithful, who will not suffer you to be tempted above that ye are able; but will... also make a way to escape, that ye may be able to bear [it].

Prov. 20:27, & 21:2 - The spirit of man [is] the candle of the LORD, searching all the inward parts of the belly. **(21:2)** - Every way of a man [is] right in his own eyes: but the LORD pondereth the hearts.

II Cor. 13:5 - Examine yourselves, whether ye be in the faith; prove your own selves. Know ye not your own selves, how that Jesus Christ is in you...

I Cor. 11:1 - Be ye followers of me, even as I also [am] of Christ.

Heb. 12:2 - Jesus the author and finisher of [our] faith; who for the joy that was set before him endured the cross, despising the shame, and is set down at the right hand of the throne of God.

Eph. 1:6-7 - To the praise of the glory of his grace, wherein he hath made us accepted in the beloved. **(7)** In whom we have redemption through his blood, the forgiveness of sins, according to the riches of his grace;

Jn. 15:12-15 - This is my commandment, That ye love one another, as I have loved you. **(13)** Greater love hath no man than this, that a man lay down his life for his friends. **(14)** Ye are my friends, if ye do whatsoever I command you. **(15)** Henceforth I call you not servants; ...but I have called you friends; for all things that I have heard of my Father I have made known unto you.

Gal. 6:10 - As we have therefore opportunity, let us do good unto all [men], especially unto them who are of the household of faith.

1 Jn. 4:19-21 - We love him, because he first loved us. **(20)** If a man say, I love God, and hateth his brother, he is a liar: for he that loveth not his brother whom he hath seen, how can he love God whom he hath not seen? **(21)** And this commandment have we from him, That he who loveth God love his brother also.

Ro. 12:10 - [Be] kindly affectioned one to another with brotherly love; in honour preferring one another;

I Cor. 4:15 - For though ye have ten thousand instructors in Christ, yet [have ye] not many fathers: for in Christ Jesus I have begotten you through the gospel.

Eph. 2:19 - ...ye are no more strangers and foreigners, but fellowcitizens with the saints, and of the household of God;

pg. 138 - II Cor. 5:7 - (For we walk by faith, not by sight:)

Phil. 4:13 - I can do all things through Christ which strengtheneth me.

Acts 15:39 - And the contention was so sharp between them, that they departed asunder one from the other: and so Barnabas took Mark,...

II Tim. 4:11 - Only Luke is with me. Take Mark, and bring him with thee: for he is profitable to me for the ministry.

Eph. 4:26 - Be ye angry, and sin not: let not the sun go down upon your wrath:

Ja. 5:16 - Confess [your] faults one to another, and pray one for another, that ye may be healed...

I Cor. 10:13 - There hath no temptation taken you but such as is common to man: but God is faithful, who will not suffer you to be tempted above that ye are able; but will with the temptation also make a way to escape, that ye may be able to bear [it].

pg. 140
Matt. 7:12 - Therefore all things whatsoever ye would that man should do to you, do you even so to them:...

Lk. 6:37 - Judge not... condemn not, and ye shall not be condemned: forgive, and ye shall be forgiven:

Ro. 12:18 & 19 - ...as much as lieth in you, live peaceably with all... **(19)** ...avenge not yourself...

Ecc. 3:1&4 - To every [thing there] is a season, and a time... **(4)** a time to weep, and a time to laugh...

pg. 141
Heb. 12:15 - lest any root of bitterness springing up trouble [you]

Ja. 3:14 - But if ye have bitter envying and strife in your hearts, glory not, and lie not against the truth.

Ps. 19:12 - Who can understand [his] errors? cleanse thou me from secret [faults].

pg. 143 - Phili. 4:8 - ...whatsoever things are true, ...honest, ...just, ...pure, ...lovely, ...of good report, ...any virtue, ...any praise, think on these things.

Lk. 17:21 - ...the kingdom of God is within you.

pg. 144- Prov. 26:5 - Answer a fool according to his folly, lest he be wise in his own conceit.

pg. 145 - Jer. 4:22 - For my people... [are] wise to do evil, but to do good they have no knowledge.

pg. 146 - Eph. 5:24 & 25 - Therefore as the church is subject unto Christ, so [let] the wives [be] to their own husbands in every thing. **(25)** Husbands, love your wives, even as Christ also loved the church, and gave himself for it;

Jas. 5:9 - Grudge not one against another,...

Prov. 17:22 - A merry heart doeth good [like] a medicine: but a broken spirit drieth the bones.

pg. 154 - I Cor. 12:4-11 - Now there are diversities of gifts, but the same Spirit. **(5)** there are differences of administrations, but the same Lord. **(6)** ...diversities of operations, but it is the same God... **(7)** But the manifestation of the Spirit is given to every man to profit withal. **(8)** For to one is given by the Spirit the word of wisdom; to another the word of knowledge **(9)** To another faith... to another the gifts of healing... **(10)** To another the working of miracles; to another prophecy; to another discerning of spirits; to another [divers] kinds of tongues; to another the interpretation of tongues: **(11)** But all these worketh that one and the selfsame Spirit... as he will.

pg. 155
Gal 5:22 & 23 - But the fruit of the Spirit is love, joy, peace, longsuffering, gentleness, goodness, faith, **(23)** Meekness, temperance, against such there is no law.

Mk. 5:30 - And Jesus... knowing... that virtue had gone out from him... said, who touched my cloths?

pg. 156
Eph. 4:11-12 - And he gave some, apostles; and some, prophets; and some, evangelists; and some, pastors and teachers; **(12)** for the perfecting of the saints... for the edifying of the body...

I Cor. 12:28 - And God hath set... in the church... apostles... prophets... teachers... miracles... gifts of healings, helps, governments... tongues.

pg. 157
Acts 8:18-20 - And when Simon saw that through laying on of the apostles' hands the Holy Ghost was given, he offered them money, **(19)** Saying, Give me also this power, that on whomsoever I lay hands, he may receive the Holy Ghost.
(20) But Peter said unto him, Thy money perish with thee, because thou hast thought that the gift of God may be purchased with money.

Is. 11:2 - And the spirit of the Lord shall rest upon him, the spirit of wisdom and understanding, the spirit of counsel and might, the spirit of knowledge and of the fear of the Lord;

Matt. 11:28-30 - Come unto me, all [ye] that labour and are heavy laden, and I will give you rest. **(29)** Take my yoke upon you, and learn of me; for I am meek and lowly in heart: and ye shall find rest unto your souls. **(30)** For my yoke is easy, and my burden is light.

Zeph. 2:3 - Seek ye the LORD, all ye meek of the earth, ...seek righteousness, seek meekness: it may be ye shall be hid in the day of the LORD'S anger.

pg. 158
I Jn. 1:8-10 - If we say that we have no sin, we deceive ourselves, and the truth is not in us. **(9)** If we confess our sins, he is faithful and just to forgive us our sins, and to cleanse us from all unrighteousness. **(10)** If we say that we have not sinned, we make him a liar, and his word is not in us.

Rev. 2:23 - ...I am he who searcheth the reins and hearts:

pg. 159
Job 35:10 - ...Where is God my maker, who giveth songs in the night;

I Sam 16:23 - And it came to pass, when the [evil] spirit from God was upon Saul, that David took an harp, and played with his hand: so Saul was refreshed, and was well, and the evil spirit departed from him.

I Thes. 4:13 & 18 - Brothers, we do not want you to be ignorant about those who fall asleep, or to grieve like the rest of men, who have no hope. **(18)** Therefore encourage each other with these words. (NIV).

pg. 160
Ro. 8:28 - And we know that all things work together for good to them that love God, to them that are the called according to [his] purpose.

pg. 161
Phili. 4:8 - ...whatsoever things are true, ...honest, ...just, ...pure, ...lovely, ...of good report, ...any virtue, ...any praise, think on these things.

X - The Setting and Format

"The Spirit of the Lord is upon me..." (Lk. 4:18).

Most counseling still takes place around a kitchen table over a cup of coffee. The various settings and formats for professional counseling can add their own flavor to the process. **A first step may be to try to acquaint a person with the setting and format in order to make them feel comfortable and secure in it.**

The government, Federal, state, and local, has offered money to religious organizations for their help with certain social services. Often the string was attached that the preaching of the gospel be curtailed. Nowadays however, the break-up and fragmentation of the family and community has intensified to crisis levels. Desperate times allow for turning to the church for help and answers. There is less money to give and fewer strings attached. Pastors may be looking for state agencies they can contact in order to refer people who come to them with problems too great for them to handle. At the same time counselors in secular agencies may be wondering what churches they can contact to refer clients to so that they might have a normal, or healthier social environment and community support network to belong to. Large state facilities are common and commonly understaffed.

There are, sadly, still intra- and inter- agency turf wars taking place and there is still an anti-religious bias in many secular social welfare systems. **Pastors should call or visit service providers before making referrals in order to find those they feel most comfortable with.** Cities often publish a directory of public and private social services. There may be a half million support groups in the country which focus on specific shared problems. There are at least ten times that number of prayer groups focused on the Lord Jesus Christ which provide help, perhaps without as much money or expertise but sometimes with more. The U.S. National Data Book (1994), reported 358,194 churches in America as of 1990.

* * * * * * * *

The setting may control the techniques used more than one's preferred counseling practice. The State may be the place of last resort for people who are poor, unwanted or "untreatable." This can result in: incarceration in a local jail or prison, short-term "revolving door" treatment, extreme chemical or drug therapy, electric shock treatment, lobotomy, or in some cases capital punishment. Public and private counseling services which can include: mental health agencies, or rehabilitation agencies, family and child services, and probation or forensic systems may do excellent work but be so extremely overloaded that money, expediency, or insurance guidelines seem to rule. It may sound like an unkind label, but many facilities are little more than a warehouse.

Only certain levels of need can be addressed and for only certain lengths of time and in a prescribed manner. A decision has to be made as to whether or not a person's discomfort merits intervention or if they will benefit from professional help at all. One estimate is that at least 25% of the people in America will need professional counseling help at some time in their life. Today there are over 5 million people in mental health institutions in this country. Instead of counseling, employed graduates of counselor education programs will likely be overseeing large or small groups.

* * * * * * * *

We are a pharmaceutically minded people. Counseling may consist solely of intense diagnosis, followed by a prescription for a drug, with casual monitoring afterward. The Valium epidemic in this country made headlines. Doctors are writing more prescriptions for medications to relieve symptoms of stress, anxiety, or depression. Chemicals are used in, or instead of, counseling. The black market in prescription drugs is estimated to be as large as the combined street traffic in crack cocaine, marijuana, and heroin. Many people are under the influence of prescription medication, either legally obtained or not.

Medical doctors (M.D., not Ph.D.) prescribe medications. If a doctor prescribed a drug people think the drug is having a healing effect. It may only be masking a problem. The medication may effect functioning and thus effect counseling if it does occur.

Combining medications can lead to a deadly interaction. **A problem presented to a physician or a counselor may be the side effect of prescribed medication which is overlooked**. Hidden substance abuse, medical problems, diet, fatigue, depression, or lack of exercise are more obvious culprits to look for.

* * * * * * * *

How we view or label a problem can effect the setting or format that is followed. Is it sin or mental illness? Is there really a problem? Some counselors, and clients as well, will avoid lengthy or painful therapy by deciding: "a marriage was not really meant to be," "they were not really in love," or "children are not adversely effected by a divorce," or "it was not really alive." Allowable excuses change over time.

This is similar to the very useful technique of reframing which refocuses attention on manageable, positive or normalizing aspects of a situation rather than on the "awfulest" possibilities. On the other hand it may only be a way to avoid responsibility or alleviate guilt for a problem no one wants to face. The same problem can be completely altered by using different labels. We do not like to endure suffering but we do like self-indulgence such as: overeating, no exercise, or a lack of self-control in general. We re-label these to make them less offensive. Is counseling needed? Is this a question of sin, or mental health, or character development? Is there a need to acquire virtues, such as temperance, wisdom, perseverance, or justice?

One example of relabeling is the "disease" model of alcoholism. Another is the term drug "addiction," Neither of these can be used as a defense in a court of law. The label "chemical imbalance" used to explain manic-depressive disorder or the "genetic" model of schizophrenia are labels misapplied to other conditions. The notion of "genetic predisposition" and widespread use of drugs seems to have superseded the systems approach toward schizophrenia which looked at the family or "system" a person lived in.

The setting can be transformed by relabeling the problems, or the characters involved. "Pastor," "counselor," “guide,” "friend," or "client," each give a different sense. This process of relabeling can be a way to ignore a problem or to make it more manageable or acceptable. Homosexuality is no longer listed as a mental illness because of intense political fighting at the American Psychological Association over its inclusion in the DSM. The reverse now takes place with gay rights activists and liberal media calling the United States a nation of "homo-phobics" (a phobia is a mental illness).

Psychological name calling is found early in church history (Matt. 3:21; Acts 12:15, & 26:24). Jesus' friends said he was “beside himself” and Paul was called “mad”. The supernatural still divides the (psychological) Sanhedrin of our day just as it did in the time of the Apostle Paul (Acts 23:6 & 9).

Someone with the zeal to build or work with God could get a "psych" label. One who has the call to speak the truth, such as a prophet, or protest song singer, could get one. The writer of a counseling book should probably also have his head examined! (Amos 3:8, Ezk. 33:32, Eph. 5:12, Ja. 3:1).

* * * * * * * * *

The church, as a center of faith, stability and healing, with caring and supporting relationships, is a setting that is itself therapeutic. The Joint Commission On Mental Health in the United states reported that 41% of people seeking psychological help sought it first at church. The church is an oasis, a place of sanctuary and refuge as well as a place of worship and center to learn of God (Ps. 27:4-5). It is also a place to fellowship with other believers, and pool resources to work together on common goals. It may have a library, a school, a recreation center, a kitchen, a day care, respite, or senior center, or other social service agency. A rescue mission is not a church but churches help support rescue missions.

Other Christian out-reaches include retreat centers for clergy and laity. There are bookstores, schools, special seminars, and TV programs. The popular radio programs of Dr. James Dobson, Joni Erikson, Chuck Swindall, Dr. Clyde Narramore, Drs. Minreth and Meier, and local call-in radio pastors, provide spiritual and mental health advice, but often without a “counseling” label.

The Church, with Her all-inclusive position may be a place where little or no counseling takes place but where a person is accepted "Just As I Am" as part of the community. This alone can help. It helps in learning healthy relationships. Or, an hallucinating schizophrenic might be viewed as a prophet, or as a demoniac needing deliverance. Someone who is undergoing great loss might be comforted, encouraged and helped, or they could be viewed as being a sinner incurring God's wrath for their lack of faith and ordered to repent (Job 16:2).

A reframing of this would be to give out a label of: "one who is being tried and tested for the purpose of character growth which may lead to responsibility, position, and blessing in the future." The suggestion here is to endure or suffer loss without seeking relief through further counseling. Overcoming obstacles and problems will develop character and reveal God's grace (Rev. 3:21).

The endurance of suffering is a major theme of the Bible (Job 23:10, Matt. 16:24, Ro. 5:3, I Cor. 13:4 & 7, Heb. 6:15, & 12:7, Jas. 1:2-3 & 5:11). Usually this refers to suffering for the Gospel, or for righteousness sake. Paul felt the goals of God outweighed any suffering but he did seek help and relief for his problems (Ro. 8:18, II Cor. 12: 8-9, Phil. 3:8). He stopped seeking help after he got an answer, not necessarily a change, from God.

Certainly the most effectual means of counseling is the anointed Word spoken by an anointed minister (Is. 10:27). In an atmosphere of Truth one of the first things to happen is that lies, chaos and confusion, doubts, fears, distractions, and petty selfishness vanish. In their place comes peace, clarity, and comfort. For many pastors counseling means simply listening, affirming, and nurturing, with "...the washing of water by the word," (Eph. 5:26). To love one another, to be in a Spiritual atmosphere, and to be Heavenly minded should be the goal of every Christian (Jn. 15:12, Ro. 8:6) but there are still areas of need to deal with (II Kgs. 4:27, Matt. 13:58).

A very common setting is short prayer counseling given right after the church service, or counseling on the run; during brief meetings, over the phone, or during visitations to homes or institutions. Some pastors refuse to counsel at all because they are opposed to it. Perhaps they believe the church services are all sufficient. There may be certain designated people or departments for handling all counseling calls. **Some pastors are simply overwhelmed, under-trained, and burned out because of counseling.** This is one of the reasons for the rise in independent Christian counseling services. These often rely on donations to survive. Insurance payment guidelines allow for payment for such services when provided by state certified counselors.

Pastoral counseling often revolves around joy and grief: weddings and funerals. Some feel marriage counseling or classes are best left till six months to a year after the wedding - when reality begins to set in. A marriage training program was described to couples planning to be married in one area. Most were on their second marriage. Over 90% endorsed the training program, but when asked if they would participate (at little or no cost) they overwhelmingly declined.

Before the wedding it may only be possible to ask about the relationship of each to God and the church, and what ceremony they want to use. It can help to go into how long they have known each other and what they think of marriage. Do the parents of both approve, and whether either party is or was married are important issues to raise. Such things as: how soon they want children, or if the bride-to-be is pregnant now, and do they have relationship and parenting skills, and how the couple will survive financially, are other important issues to explore – if possible.

In the context of the setting and format it is important to point out that grief counseling may be needed after any loss; not only divorce, death, and illness. It should not be assumed which people are involved and how severely they are affected. It may not be just the individual with the problem or their immediate family. Siblings and friends may be ignored but they may need comfort and counseling as much as the parents of a deceased child.

Some communities offer counseling to the entire class or school after a student's suicide in order to prevent additional attempts by others. Some cities have an entire school set aside for children who had someone in their family murdered. Grief may be expressed strongly at the hospital, hospice, church, school, funeral home, or graveyard. Grief counseling may be needed anywhere and at any time, even years after an incident. People from different cultures have different ways, and times, of reacting.

* * * * * * * * *

The group model is often used for people with grief issues to resolve. It has been found to be an effective way to utilize the empathy and experience of people who have any similar problems. In addition to grief it is utilized for the survivors and perpetrators of incest, rape, other crimes, eating disorders, divorce, unemployment, cancer patients, those with other serious illnesses, and many other issues. It is more cost and time effective than one on one counseling though most therapists use a combination of the two.

Some problems have been so well studied that the most effective types of counseling to date are known. This is a contribution of an academic or scientific approach - the compiling of sufficient clinical data so as to be able to draw conclusions about treatment. Groups are considered the best method for working with people with substance abuse problems and also for helping their families.

Substance abuse is often kept secret by controlling, lying, and manipulative behavior. The counselor can be fooled by an "expert" client. A group of peer "experts," if they are actively participating, see through each other's ploys to not: talk, feel, or trust. They can stop one another from avoiding dealing with their problems and help each other learn how to relate in a healthy way.

The groups of Alcoholics Anonymous have long been using church facilities even while they deny the exclusive claims of Jesus Christ (Jn. 17:3, Acts 4:12). They relabel Deity: "God as you understand him." A co-founder, Bill Wilson, described the principles of AA as being "ancient and universal ones, the common property of mankind." To be more precise, their principles and practices stem from the Holy Bible.

Traditional adult Sunday school classes have also been transformed into a series of groups meeting around particular problems. The growth of these groups, and the churches that sponsor them, have in some cases been spectacular. Pastors and church members not participating in the groups may feel threatened by the shift in emphasis. The group, like the church itself, becomes a substitute or surrogate extended family. The relationships formed are strong and may seem to be in direct competition to the unity of the church family or to what some members believe are its primary purpose or message.

It takes more than one semester or Sunday school year to deal with all that surfaces. **The mission of the Church and even a definition of mental health requires more than just looking inward at self and one's own relationships.** The balance between counseling or self-help groups and any other activities may rest on an ever changing measure of the urgency of the problem and allowable labels.

* * * * * * * * *

Agencies to contact for information or help include: the Catholic Charities, Lutheran Social Services, the Salvation Army, the rescue mission or a united churches aid program in your area, or a local church. The World Health Organization, of the United Nations, the National Institute of Health, the National Center for Disease Control, and the U. S. Census Bureau, and Labor Department, or other Federal government agencies all give away information. Local state, county, and city agencies can be helpful.

Universities and colleges are good places to find information. Names of agencies may begin with: "The Federal...," "The American...," or "The National...," or use the state, county or city name, i.e. "The New York Lighthouse for the Blind," or "Wayne County Association for people with Developmental or cognitive impairments," or "Toledo United Churches." Telephone directory assistance can give an 800 number. A reference librarian can find an address.

The name of the agency may be the name of the problem such as: "the Pain Management Center," or "Alcoholics Anonymous," or the "Multiple Sclerosis Foundation," or "the Eating Disorders Clinic," or "the Mental Health Center." "Word of mouth," or referrals by clergy, law enforcement agencies, schools, local hospitals, or a family physician can help direct a search. Local newspaper, radio, or TV, news editors can too. Bible believing Christians work in church run and secular agencies. There are also professional social workers and counselors who are antagonistic toward Christianity.

CHAPTER X REVIEW

Where does your counseling take place? Describe it in terms of: amount of time, number of sessions, how it is labeled, and how the people involved are labeled. Is there a fee structure? Do you have a choice in these things or do you feel forced into a particular format or setting? What steps can be taken to bring choice back in?

In the book of Matthew, chapter 28, verse 19, the RSV, NIV, NAS, and the NKJ versions say: "...make disciples of all nations...." The King James version says "teach all nations...." What is the difference, in setting and format, between teaching and the making of disciples? Are these just different labels for the same thing? How does counseling compare or fit in with these categories or other labels?

(Scripture references for chapter X)

pg. 169

Luke 4:18 - The Spirit of the Lord [is] upon me, because he hath anointed me to preach the gospel to the poor; he hath sent me to heal the brokenhearted, to preach deliverance to the captives, and recovering of sight to the blind, to set at liberty them that are bruised,

pg. 173

Matt. 3:21 - and when his friends heard of it, they went out to lay hold of him, for the said, He is beside himself.

Acts 12:15 - And they said unto her, Thou art mad. But she constantly affirmed that it was even so. Then said they, It is his angel.

Acts 26:24 - And as he thus spake for himself, Festus said with a loud voice, Paul... much learning doth make thee mad.

Acts 23:6 & 9 - ...Paul...cried out...of the hope and resurrection of the dead I am called in question. **(9)** ... if a spirit or an angel hath spoken to him, let us not fight against God.

pg. 174

Amos 3:8 - The lion hath roared, who will not fear? the Lord GOD hath spoken, who can but prophesy?

Ezek. 33:32 - And, lo, thou [art] unto them as a very lovely song of one that hath a pleasant voice, and can play well on an instrument: for they hear thy words, but they do them not.

Eph. 5:12 - For it is a shame even to speak of those things which are done of them in secret.

Ja. 3:1 - My brethren, be not many masters, knowing that we shall receive the greater condemnation.

Ps. 27:4-5 - One thing have I desired of the Lord, that will I seek after; that I may dwell in the house of the Lord all the days of my life, to behold the beauty of the Lord, and to inquire in his temple. **(5)** For in the time of trouble he shall hide me in his pavilion: in the secret of his tabernacle shall he hide me; he shall set me up upon a rock.

pg.175
Job 16:2 - I have heard many such things: miserable comforters [are] ye all.

Rev. 3:21 - To him that overcometh will I grant to sit with me in my throne, even as I also overcame, and am set down with my Father in his throne.

Job 23:10 - But he knoweth the way that I take: [when] he hath tried me, I shall come forth as gold.

Matt. 16:24 - ...if any [man] will come after me, let him deny himself and take up his cross, and follow me.

Ro. 5:3 - ...we glory in tribulations... knowing ...tribulation worketh patience;

I Cor. 13:4 & 7 - Charity suffereth long, and is kind... **(7)** Beareth all things... endureth all things...

Heb. 6:15 - And so, after he had patiently endured, he obtained the promise.

Heb. 12:7 - If ye endure chastening, God dealeth with you as with sons...

Jas. 1: 2-3 & 5:11 - ...count it all joy when you fall into ... temptations; **(3)** ...the trying of your faith worketh patience. **(11)** Behold, we count them happy which endure.

Ro. 8:18 - For I reckon that the sufferings of this present time are not worthy [to be compared] with the glory which shall be revealed in us.

II Cor. 12: 8-9 - For this thing I besought the Lord thrice that it might depart from me. **(9)** And he said unto me, My grace is sufficient for thee: for my strength is made perfect in weakness...

Phil. 3:8 - ...I count all things [but] loss for the excellency of the knowledge of Christ Jesus my Lord: for whom I have suffered the loss of all things and do count them [but] dung, that I may win Christ.

pg.176 - Is. 10:27 - ...his burden shall be taken away from off thy shoulder, and his yoke from off thy neck, and the yoke shall be destroyed because of the anointing.

Eph. 5:26 - That he may sanctify and cleanse it by the washing of water by the word,

Jn. 15:12 - ...love one another...

Ro. 8:6 - For to be carnally minded [is] death; but to be spiritually minded [is] life and peace.

II Kings 4:27 - And when she came to the man of God... she caught him by the feet: ... And the man of God said, ...her soul [is] vexed within her: and the LORD hath hid [it] from me, and hath not told me.

Matt. 13:58 - And he did not many mighty works there because of their unbelief.

pg. 179 - Jn. 17:3 - ...this is life eternal, that they might know thee, the only true God and Jesus Christ, whom thou hast sent.

Acts 4:12 - Neither is there salvation in any other: for there is none other name given under heaven, whereby we must be saved.

XI - Guidelines

*"Where no counsel is the people fall:
but in the multitude of counsellors
there is safety." (Pro. 11:14).*

Jethro told Moses to select "men of truth" to help him (Ex. 18:21). Accuracy of facts or truths alone may not change anyone's mind or life. It is possible to be 100% correct and still be dead wrong. The Apostle Paul's words had both "truth and reason" (Acts 26:25). Jesus is full of grace and truth (John 1:14). God graciously accommodates us beyond truth.

The decision to comfort or confront rests on several factors the Bible mentions in connection with truth. These include: "speaking the truth in love" (Eph. 4:15), "mercy and truth" (Ps. 85:10), "grace and truth" (Jn. 1:14), "in spirit and in truth" (Jn. 4:23), under the guidance of "The Spirit of Truth" (Jn. 16:13), who is the Holy Spirit. There may first need to be: "truth in the inward parts" (Ps. 51:6), and growth of the desire to "love the truth" (Zech. 8:19), before God can "Sanctify ...through (His) truth..." (Jn. 17:17).

This would seem to be simple since Jesus is the "Truth" (Jn. 14:6). However, a couple on the verge of divorce may sound like the voice of Pilate asking: "what is truth?" (Jn. 18:38). They scream the answer at each other: "crucify him (or her)." Some counselors consider they are just teaching, but that takes finesse.

It would be a grave error of judgement to assume that by reading a description or discussion of counseling techniques one is thereby qualified to apply them. Another well known American trait is the desire for instant everything. This is not only for instant coffee and microwave dinners. It is also for quick cures or easy answers to problems and damaging habits that have built up over years.

In the article: "They Had To Beg Us To Pray: Reflections on the undesirability of Clinical Pastoral Education," Dr. Gary Ahiskog notes that a Pastor/counselor should at least be able to recognize the difference between: psychoses (20% of likely case-loads), personality disorders, (30%), and problems of living (50%). (The Journal of Pastoral Care, 1993, Vol. 47, #2, 179-187). Knowing some basic Bible doctrines and Christian morality would also help. Having a few simple techniques and spiritual discernment would likely be of great value as well. And praying helps too.

* * * * * * * *

The prescribed course for a counselor is 4 years of undergraduate work and 2 to 4 years of graduate study. Most professional counseling is done by people with an M.S.W., M.R.C., M.A., or M.S.; a seminary level degree (M.Div.), not a doctor, Ph.D., or Ed.D., or psychiatrist, (M.D.). Even with the degrees there are several 8 hour exams to take, and 2 to 4 years of supervised counseling required, before being allowed to hang up a shingle as a counselor in most states.

A Christian counselor should have 2 to 4 years of Bible college or seminary as well. Chaplains might want a year of supervised Clinical Pastoral Education (C.P.E.) or the equivalent (if they included prayer). All of this will include reading (and writing papers on) at least 100 lengthy textbooks, and at least that many shorter works, and 10 times that number of primary sources such as journal articles. The people, theories, and techniques mentioned in this book can likely all be found on the Internet for further study.

As Paul Harvey put it: "now you know the rest of the story" (Ecc. 7:16, 12:12). So again, for the third time, be aware that this book is not going to answer all questions and problems nor can it make the reader into a counselor. What can be learned from any book are suggestions to try and help with: *diagnosis* - describing the problem, *prognosis* - the usual or expected course and end of the problem, and hints at *intervention, treatment, and referral.*

* * * * * * * *

Whatever the training, there are limits to what can be accomplished. We still need laws, prisons, and funerals. It is important to have counseling guidelines that include boundaries and limits and the ability to say "no," or "make an appointment," or "I cannot help you." These help effectively manage caseloads and avoid counselor burnout. Other helpful aids are: pastor and/or counselor support groups, retreat weekends, vacations, regular exercise, hobbies, interests other than care giving, and changing jobs.

These help maintain both perspective and effectiveness. Lifeguards must protect themselves from being pulled under by a drowning person. Counselors too must learn to protect and fight for their own mental and spiritual health. It may help to use an answering machine or disconnect the phone to guard family times such as during meals.

> The State has emptied its mental health institutions amid promises of funding, for local community support systems that has barely if ever materialized. This has resulted in a flood of needy people in our cities. Much wisdom is required to avoid being overwhelmed and given a mission other than the one(s) the church chooses for itself (Zech. 8:23, Matt. 22:14 & 26:11, & Rev. 12:15).

Most states have laws that govern both religious and secular counseling practice. Ethical behavior, including such things as disclosure or confidentiality, is legislated. Many states require disclosure where there is a threat to the safety of another individual or the client such as in the case of suspected child abuse. Failure to disclose when it is required or breaking confidentiality when it is not appropriate may be a misdemeanor punishable by: a fine, the loss of license, and the privilege to practice, and imprisonment. Pastors and churches, as well as secular counselors, can be sued and should have malpractice insurance.

According to the Bureau of Labor Statistics, in 2014, the average salary in America is slightly over $40,000. The average for a counselor is $45,000 and for a pastor of a large church $95,000. Therapy may range, from 5 to 50, one hour sessions at between $35 and $100 each session. Pastors may do this without compensation beyond their wage or church volunteers may be called on.

Depression may come from many sources and may in fact be part of the healing or grieving process and thus should be allowed rather than fixed. Other types of depression respond well to involvement with any activity. A workout at a gym or going to dinner with friends may help lift it. Depression may also be one of the side effects of medication. Certain medications can reduce it. Again, it matters how we label it.

* * * * * * * *

Counseling requires good judgement and involves risk. Problem situations may become even more intense, before they get better, because the counselor is upsetting the status quo. It can be devastating to have a client commit suicide or kill someone else, not to mention "lesser" failures.

If a counselor (or anyone) suspects a client may commit suicide the counselor should clearly broach the subject. Ask: "have you thought about killing yourself?" The next questions should be aimed at finding out if there are realistic plans and/or actual materials available for an attempt.

The counselor should keep talking with the individual at least until other help arrives or: 1) the plans are renounced, and 2) any materials (pills, guns, car keys etc.) that might be used are relinquished, and 3) the client agrees not to attempt suicide without contacting the counselor or other specified support person first. If this is not agreed to the counselor should call the police (dial O, or 911) and have the person arrested or committed as surely as if they said they had a gun and were going to shoot someone.

* * * * * * * *

I visited the District Attorney on behalf of a young man attending my church who had been arrested for burglary. What a surprise to learn that his prior arrest record included robbing the home of the first pastor who had tried to help him. I have to confess to being thankful that I was the second pastor on that case not the first.

My work in a Psychiatric Center and a Sheltered Workshop has given me training with some of the most seriously broken and disturbed people in our society. It has also required being vaccinated against Hepatitis which is a contagious disease hospital workers may get. Hepatitis, Tuberculosis, Aids, and other contagious diseases make visitation in hospices, hospitals, and prisons a high risk ministry just as working with lepers was at one time - and still is in some places. We have vaccinations and cures– but not for everything.

Some hospitals may attempt to control what ministers share with patients. They have no legal right to do so but discretion is often called for (Pro. 19:11). On the other hand there are some Christians who think hospital visitation is for evangelization rather than comfort care and encouragement. They want to challenge the way a suffering patient expresses his or her faith in God - to make sure they are saved. Job's comforters!

* * * * * * * *

Asking the right questions (at the right time) is often good counseling. These are not always profound or revealing questions. A counselor may want to avoid opening a can of worms. The best question to ask will prompt an answer that can be dealt with. Instead of asking what a person's problem is, it may be better to ask: "is there something I can help you bring to the cross?" "Do you need help in leaving something at the cross?" These type of questions clearly show the direction and help available.

Most theories regard client motivation as crucial to a positive outcome. Some counselors think it is critical. The first step is to build a relationship, instill hope, and have the patient's emotional involvement in working on and resolving the problem situation (Pro. 13:12). This may even be the only requirement for counseling or it may be a way to start and maintain it. An atmosphere of warmth and acceptance may work well with some clients. Others prefer a more formal, even a clinical relationship.

Fees can demonstrate or even help create commitment, as can place and time limits, schedules, and homework. It may help to accompany a client into a real-life setting to observe him or her, or to help with a homework assignment. Homework may also consist of making self-monitoring reports to clarify a person's situation, or level or type of thinking, or it can be tasks that in themselves produce change.

Counseling requires the ability to focus on one's own thoughts and behavior. If a client cannot, or appears to refuse to self-reflect and resists becoming self-aware many counselors will discontinue therapy. Refusal to carry out simple assignments is another reason to drop a client. Counseling is not for everyone. A person who comes for counsel because a court, or their spouse, family, or boss, require it, may just "play along" but passively resist any change or self-disclosure.

* * * * * * * *

A common model for pastors is to allow three to five private counseling sessions before referring a person to others in the church or to outside agency specialists. Some people go to another church for counsel, perhaps to "save face," or perhaps to find any help at all. Some pastors will only counsel someone of the opposite sex when a third party is present. In view of the many scandals that have surfaced this is a good policy if there are mature third parties available.

Feelings should not be the only measure of success. Instead, *concrete goals* can be established and worked on. Goals should be clear enough so that success and termination can be evaluated by both the therapist and client. These can be: simple symptom or problem reduction, help with major life changes, personality changes, or growth and self-fulfillment. Writing a contract or outline can help. Creating obtainable short-term goals can help motivate a person to overcome feelings.

* * * * * * * *

Some problems require lifelong maintenance. A person may not stay long enough to learn what the problem is. Americans move often. It can be easier to work through a cognitive limitation, or a physical disability, or a sensory impairment, than to work with a person with emotional problems, or relationship problems. It is not difficult to teach a person who is slow, or blind to wear appropriate clothing, or to teach a person who uses a wheelchair to plan ahead when going somewhere that is not wheelchair accessible.

This may be easier than teaching those who lack appropriate emotional responses or motives. They may not see or feel them as reasonable, real or necessary. They can however, learn to modify their behavior according to the needs of others rather than to only respond to their own needs and impulses. Instead of repeatedly teaching the importance of considering others, other motivators must be found.

Forgiveness is often taught as self-interest; being for the good of the one who forgives, rather than for reconciliation of relations between people. People with Borderline personality disorder are masters at manipulating, often creating great frustration and rage in people trying to help them. They may always be looking for the "perfect parent(s)." They know how to elevate and build up the ones they choose to idealize but will turn and dash them to pieces when they do not get what they want, which is often. They may telephone their pastor or counselor repeatedly day and night to confirm their reality. They usually have had many counselors and failed attempts at therapy so they know "all the ropes," and terminology. They may feign a suicide attempt in order to get attention and thus be rescued again. Unfortunately they may "accidentally" succeed in the attempt.

* * * * * * * *

Not all abused children grow up to be cult leaders or members but many do tend to gravitate to the love manifested by the church (Ps. 27:10, Ps. 68:6). Our innate spiritual hunger makes the offer of God's unconditional love alluring to all, especially for those who are starved for any love at all. People who have never been nurtured may not know what it is, or how to comfort or support themselves internally let alone nurture anyone else. Helping others can help one's own mental health. Nurturing others teaches one how to nurture oneself. It may help to create a way to practice this or to confirm a person's belief in his or her own ability to love and to be loved.

A simple rule, ignored by many systems, both secular and religious, is that with all interventions: psychological, medical, or spiritual, ample feedback and careful long term monitoring are essential for determining the veracity and the endurance of any effect. **Studies of all types of secular counseling show it is effective in about 30% to 60% of the cases**. One report of miracle ministries of the 1950's and 60's was that about 2% (that is millions) of the reported miracles were real and lasted.

When a new program or system opens it may begin with enormously high statistics on its success or cure rate, sometimes as high as 99% or 100%. This may be due to taking only a selective group of people to work with, but it is also because it takes several years before relapses and failures can be factored into the statistics. Our American system requires expensive advertisement and positive success stories for a program (or a book on counseling) to attract customers and support.

Often in counseling a person's problems will not be solved or "fixed." The individual is simply helped to regain some perspective or momentum for carrying their own problems. In other words, **his or her faith is renewed.** Even real "fixes" are temporary. Everyone (except Enoch and Elijah), who has ever lived or been healed, whether by a miracle or by medicine, has eventually died, or will die, unless the Lord returns before they do.

One goal of Existential therapists is to point out the difference between normal and neurotic problems. In our pampered society there are some who seek counseling because they do not even know what is essential for life and happiness. Mere inconvenience may be labeled tragedy. There may be ignorance or uncertainty about what is a normal or an appropriate human response, (let alone a spiritual one), in an unfamiliar situation. There may be inability, or ignorance of how, to make it.

The mislabeling of: repression, re-direction, dissociation, "the existential moment," "accidents," or other natural phenomena is another, often made, intellectual error. These erroneously get called supernatural experiences. The natural man wants to either deny the spiritual, or own and control it.

One hundred and fifty years ago the American poet and Existentialist Ralph Waldo Emerson responded thus:

"I laugh at the lore of the learned clan.
At the high brow looks of the Sophist band,
For what are they all in their proud conceit,
When God and man at the bush may meet."

The two most frequent requests for guidance regarding the supernatural are: **"How can I be led of God?" and "How can I truly know the leading is from the Lord?"**

An answer similar to just the time required to become a secular counselor would be: "wait on God, and study the Bible for 10 to 12 years, while living and working with people who do know the voice and ways of God." Moses waited 40 years, Jesus waited 30 years, and Paul waited 14 years, for a supernatural ministry. Do we care to wait?

Many Christians need to first learn common sense and politeness. Why do we put up with prophets who use their gifts to steal members from other churches, or to get money, or to wrongly influence, or for power? They should be avoided like the plague. Those who violate privacy by revealing the secrets of the heart, but have no real word from the Lord, flaunt their gifts, but are simply being rude. They could not succeed in this arrogance if people did not want a "king" over them: Blue Cross and Blue Shield plus a pastor with the gifts of healing.

This misuse of offices and gifts is also possible because some people have had an abusive background and consider it normal to be misused. They first need a natural sense of right and wrong. Such confusion and an over trusting attitude could be cured by reading the Bible. It records that Prophets can lie (I Kgs. 13:18), Apostles may fight among themselves (Acts. 15:39, Gal. 2:11), and even God is jealous and gets angry (Deut. 16:15, Mk. 3:5)! We tend to give too much authority and deference to medical doctors and counselors too.

An awareness of the manifest presence of God may require a specific grace, an unusual outpouring or release of the Holy Spirit, or the cultivation and growth of spiritual senses. The Bible gives guidance for cultivating God's presence (Jer. 29:13). It warns of counterfeits, imitators, and mockers, of the presence of God, or of spiritual senses, gifts, fruit, and offices. (Deut. 13:1-3, & 18:20-22, Mk. 13:22, Acts 13:6-11, II Pet. 2:12). There have long been those who try to fake spirituality as a learned technique without the grace of God to empower. The seven sons of Sceva failed at an exorcism sham and paid dearly for (Acts 19:14-16).

It is not always possible to discern grace by a person's behavior, even for someone in a spiritual office, such as a Pastor. Real spiritual functioning may continue in a person's life even when he or she is not living in obedience to the Lord. These operations may also be present to some degree among those who love the Lord but who do not acknowledge the gifts, or do not display those mannerisms that are commonly associated with the supernatural.

Anger, bitterness, and double mindedness, may prevent someone from receiving the grace of God. These cause resistance in counseling too (Heb. 3:8). Even when Prevenient or Common grace, Specific grace, or Christian grace are truly present there may still be a need for further teaching or counseling. A change in environment and associates often occurs or is called for, voluntarily or maybe not.

A secular counselor may help a Christian by claiming ignorance of spiritual things and offering to deal with "natural" problems. A pastor or Christian counselor has a greater task in trying to restore or maintain a person's walk with the Lord. The one has only to tell the difference between the healthy and the sick. The other is charged with discerning the Holy from the profane: the spiritual from the natural (Ezk. 44:23). Natural "happiness" comes from happenings that change. "Joy" comes from knowing the Lord Jesus who never changes.

When a person has a spiritual rebirth and infilling or renewing of the Holy Spirit there is someone new to work with (Tit. 3:5). The work of emotional healing may happen instantly with a damaged personality being completely replaced by a whole one. More often however, it takes place over time by the application of daily help from God and from people. Instant healing, change, or growth, centered around the indwelling life of Jesus Christ, the perfect model and guide, is possible but others may participate in this work over time. This creates the miracle of patience and compassion.

* * * * * * * *

It is difficult to give a full understanding of faith over the limited time of TV, radio, or even in pulpit messages and books. Counsel is given that sounds like sound bites, clichés, slogans, or commercials. Some of the hardest, most profound questions get asked 30 seconds before it is time to leave a meeting.

We expect quick easy answers, tweets and twitters. I recently received a disappointing medical report. A friend I shared it with said: "that's rough, I'm sorry to hear it, I'll be praying for you." That was simple but sufficient. Someone else began to tell me all the "spiritual" rules I should follow. These were supposed to get me out of my condition or help me avoid problems. Another one of Job's comforters!

One Christmas I enjoyed watching as a little child in her daddy's arms touched her nose every time the lights on the tree blinked on. When she took her hand off her face, the lights went off. She tried other people's faces too and had a great time being in control of the flow of electricity. An amusing story is told about the natives on the Pacific islands during W.W. II. They watched as the Americans cut air fields in the jungle and then huge planes came and brought loads of supplies. The natives figured out how it worked. They cut air fields in the jungle too in what became known as the "Cargo Cults." Surprise! Nothing happened.

Today people still observe what takes place around Real Faith and then try to imitate those peripheral events by creating rules of what to say and do to activate faith or twist God's arm (Matt. 15:9) or deny such things are real or possible at all. They may get offended if their superstitions are questioned. However, remember, God blessed Job when he prayed for his "friends" (Job 42:10).

Popular "faith" messages would be a lot closer to the truth if we substituted the word "hope" for "faith" (Ro. 8:24), or if we stopped to ask what God thought about the situation rather than demanding our own way. God does not fit our formulas (even mine). He does use simple and foolish things to confound the wise. However, when we make them into rules we are pretending to be wise in spiritual matters and He no longer jumps through our hoops. It is important to keep in mind that healings and miracles are secondary to the main purposes of God.

In addition to moving in other gifts I have laid hands on and prayed for people who were sick or dying. One result has been complete restoration beyond any medical expectation. Other times the results have only been the cessation of pain. Many times there were no discernible results at all. Often though, there is an impartation of faith in God that serves to strengthen and help people bear their own burdens, or to go directly to God themselves.

These are signs and wonders pointing to a Spiritual reality which has as its aim eternal things - that we might be transformed into the image of Jesus Christ, the Son of God, who chose to only do the will of the Father. This is hard to consider when we are faced with crisis or pain. This is about power and control and people have always fought over those things. It helps to remember Our Lord faced the cross and prayed to his Father God, “Thy will be done.”

Three final guidelines, to briefly consider, can apply to both Christian and secular counselors. Like many points in this book, *transference, voyeurism, and cynicism,* could use a full chapter each, just to define. They may need a complete book, and several graduate college courses to fully cover.

Transference refers to the counselor taking on the appearance of a significant person in the client's life. For example, a man may be perceived in the role of "father," or "brother," or "husband." Counter-transference occurs when the counselor sees the client in the reciprocal role as a: child, sibling, or spouse. This is useful for examining the types of relationships that existed and now need to be repaired. These counseling relationships can be very strong. It is unethical for a counselor to use this to fulfill his or her own emotional needs. The relationship is temporary. This is not your family. In the end everyone goes their own separate ways.

Voyeurism presents another trap. Here it refers to excessive curiosity, not the dictionary meaning of the word. It is easy to be engrossed with gossip; to always be looking for, or living to be involved with, problems. People's lives and problems are interesting, even compelling. To stay healthy we must deliberately turn our eyes elsewhere. Look to: God, or our own families, to ourselves, and look at the strengths and success of others, not their problems. This book is all about problems, but living with that focus is unhealthy.

Another trap counselors fall into is to think everyone is dishonest, has severe problems, selfish motives, or that there is no hope. Most of us want to appear basically normal, to "pass." Complete cold-blooded self-appraisal, or total honesty about a problem is rare. People often only come to a counselor when their problems reach crisis level. They may be too angry to want help. Nothing short of a miracle will help then.

These things breed cynicism. Hospital care givers may think everyone is going to get a severe illness. Only 5-10% will. Nursing home workers may think everyone will be disabled when they get older, only 5-10% will. Most people manage their own lives, with only a support system of family, friends, church and their neighborhood. This works well without any professional counseling. In normal circumstances most people will be honest and unselfish. Even so, all people need the Lord. He is our hope.

* * * * * * * *

This book is not an attempt to create a new "Christian Psychology." It only describes theories and practices and compares them with scripture. In order not to diminish the spiritual or confuse it with the natural I choose to emphasize, as the Apostle Paul did, that **the union of the Spirit of God and the rebirth of God's spirit in man is a mystery. That mystery and the sovereignty of God are the most important guidelines–for life and for counseling.**

CHAPTER XI REVIEW

One guideline to note is about this book. It contains brief descriptions of things that could be covered in whole chapters and books. Some of them need to be repeated, practiced, or experienced year after year for the concept to be well understood. Do not worry about any point that is difficult to relate to, This is especially true in regard to the functioning of spiritual senses, gifts, fruit and offices. Without first hand experience with the real thing we are prone to have misconceptions and doubts.

This book is to be used for self-reflection. With this chapter the questions to ask are: "do I have guidelines?" "What are they?" "Have I run into trouble, or seen someone else have difficulty, because of violating a guideline?" "What are some pressures that cause me to ignore guidelines?" "Can I gently but forcibly say '"no,"' and enforce it?" "What do I feel like, and what can I do about my feelings, when I impose a boundary or limit?"

I have seen secular and Christian counselors, and pastors and prophets, intimidate or bully a person into giving them the sort of response they wanted. They then leave, feeling their counsel or ministry was successful, when in fact it was not. How do you feel about, and deal with, time restraints, and long term problems, or failures?

A fast food chain lured customers in by offering free refills on coffee. To limit the requests for refills they heated the coffee much higher than normal. They warned their staff to be careful with it - but not their customers. One sued after being severely burned and won because the company's fraud came to light. Politicians distorted this in order to attack the court system. They ranted at those who lacked self-control and made others pay for it. Those who make money by creating unsafe environments do not want to be held responsible. A well-known guideline on lies and denial in this country is *caveat emptor*, "buyer beware."

(Scripture references for chapter XI)

pg. 185 - Prov. 11:14 - Where no counsel [is], the people fall: but in the multitude of counsellors [there is] safety.

Ex. 18:21 - Moreover thou shall provide... men of truth...

Acts 26:25 - ...but speak the words of truth and reason. (NKJ)

Eph. 4:15 - But speaking the truth in love,...

Ps. 85:10 - Mercy and truth are met together;...

Jn. 1:14, 4:23, 16:13 - **(14)** And the Word was... full of grace and truth. **(23)** ...worship the Father in spirit and in truth...**(13)** - ...when he, the Spirit of truth, is come...

Ps. 51:6 - Behold, thou desirest truth in the inward parts:

Zech. 8:19 - ...love the truth and peace.

Jn. 17:17 - Sanctify them through thy truth: thy word is truth.

Jn. 14:6, 18:38 - Jesus saith.. "I am... the truth,... **(38)** Pilate saith... What is truth?

pg. 187
Ecc. 7:16 & 12:12 - Be not righteous over much; neither make thyself over wise: why shouldest thou destroy thyself? **(12)** - ...of making many books [there is] no end; and much study [is] a weariness of the flesh.

pg. 188
Zech. 8:23 - Thus saith the LORD of hosts; In those days [it shall come to pass], that ten men shall take hold out of all languages of the nations, even shall take hold of the skirt of him that is a Jew, saying, We will go with you: for we have heard... God [is] with you.

Matt. 22:14 & 26:11 - For many are called, but few [are] chosen. **(11)** - For ye have the poor always with you; but me ye have not always.

Rev. 12:15 - And the serpent cast out of his mouth water as a flood after the woman, that he might cause her to be carried away of the flood.

pg. 191
Pro. 19:11, 13:12 - The discretion of a man deferreth his anger; and [it is] his glory to pass over a transgression. **(12)** Hope deferred maketh the heart sick: but [when] the desire cometh, [it is] a tree of life.

pg. 194
Ps. 27:10 & 68:6 - When my father and my mother forsake me... the Lord will take me up. **(6)** - God setteth the solitary in families:

pg. 197 - I Kgs. 13:18 - ...[But] he (the prophet) lied to him.

Acts 15:39 - the contention was so sharp between them that they parted asunder one from the other.

Gal. 2:11 - But when Peter was come to Antioch I withstood him to the face because he was to be blamed.

Deut. 16:15 - (For the LORD thy God is a jealous God...
the anger of the LORD thy God...

Mk. 3:5 - he... looked... on them with anger, being grieved...

pg. 198
Jer, 29:13 - And ye shall seek me, and find me, when ye shall search for me with all your heart.

Deut. 13:1-3 - If... a prophet... giveth thee a sign or a wonder... **(2)** And the sign or wonder come to pass... (and) he spake unto thee saying, Let us go unto other Gods... **(3)** Thou shalt not hearken unto the words of that prophet...

Deut. 18:20-22 - But the prophet, which shall presume to speak a word in my name, which I have not commanded... or... speak in the name of other gods... shall die. **(21)** ...How shall we know the word which the LORD hath not spoken? **(22)** When a prophet speaketh in the name of the LORD, if the thing follow not, nor come to pass, that [is] the thing which the LORD hath not spoken, ...the prophet hath spoken it presumptuously...

Mk. 13:22 - For false Christs and false prophets shall rise, and shall shew signs and wonders, to seduce... the elect.

Acts 13:6-11 - ...they found a certain sorcerer, a false prophet...**(7)** ...Sergius Paulus ...called for Barnabas and Saul, and desired to hear the word of God. **(8)** But Elymas the sorcerer... withstood them... **(9)** Then Saul... filled with the Holy Ghost, set his eyes on him, **(10)** And said,...[thou]

child of the devil... wilt thou not cease to pervert the right ways of the Lord? **(11)** And now, behold, the hand of the Lord [is] upon thee, and thou shalt be blind, not seeing the sun for a season.

II Pet. 2:12 - But these, as natural brute beasts, made to be taken and destroyed, speak evil of the things that they understand not; and shall utterly perish in their own corruption;

Acts 19:14-16 - And there were seven sons of [one] Sceva, ...which did so. **(15)** And the evil spirit answered and said, Jesus I know, and Paul I know; but who are ye? **(16)** And the man in whom the evil spirit was leaped on them and overcame them...

Heb. 3:8 - Harden not your hearts, as in the provocation, in the day of temptation in the wilderness:

pg. 199
Ezk. 44:23 - And they shall teach my people [the difference] between the holy and the profane, and cause them to discern between the unclean and the clean.

Titus 3:5 - ...he saved us, by the washing of regeneration, and the renewing of the Holy Ghost;

pg. 200
Matt. 15:9 - But in vain they do worship me, teaching [for] doctrines the commandments of men.

Job 42:10 - And the LORD turned the captivity of Job, when he prayed for his friends...

pg. 201
Ro. 8:24 - For we are saved by hope:

XII - Summary and Conclusion

"...Fear God and keep his commandments..." (Ecc. 12:13).

Jethro said to Moses, in regard to the advice he gave him: "if thou shalt do this thing, *and God commands thee so*, then thou shalt be able to endure, and all this people shall also go to their place in peace" (Ex. 18:23). God later confirms his advice on a spiritual level (Num. 11:17). The question will arise as to whether or not something mentioned in this book should be pursued and studied further. For this, there must be a sense of God's leading, *"...and God commands thee so."*

Since the "grand theorizing" of Freud and Jung different schools of psycho-therapy have emerged. Many studied or worked in a psychoanalytical framework but developed their own systems as a reaction against the Freudian model or simply to find more effective ways to help people. Others wanted to include a Christian, or spiritual perspective to what they believed was a "scientific" framework. Freudian psychoanalysis averages $220,000 and many years of therapy to complete. It was said of Freud that despite his theories on pathology and treatment he gave out an enormous amount of advice between the couch and the door - which may be why he had any success.

Today counseling is still advice giving. It is also detective work which asks: "what are basic human commonalities, and how do we differ from one another?" It also asks: "why do we develop such destructive ways of being, and why do people resist changing?"

Some theorists have focused their attention on how we think and feel, even considering the two identical. Others look at how we behave and learn, or focus on how we communicate, relate, and perceive ourselves. Their views overlap and their counseling techniques may overlap because they are looking at the same thing - we humans.

The problems may result from: burdens from the past, either known or forgotten, or habits that need to be learned or unlearned, or difficulties with our environment and culture today. Reduction to just these few areas does not make the search for solutions easy, just easier. Multiply these by each individual's unique life and it gets complicated.

A counselor must ask: "what is the problem and what is preventing the person from solving it?" *(Diagnosis.)*. We need to consider what the expected course or end of the situation is. How serious or pressing is the problem? *(Prognosis.)* What can be done to remove hindrances or blocks? What does the person need to live and grow to his or her fullest? *(Intervention or treatment.)*

Other important questions are: "is this within the scope of my experience and expertise, and am I the right counselor, or should I refer this person to someone else?" The issues raised in this book give an indication of just some of the questions we might want to ask. We need to go beyond this medical model. It can be helpful but it does not give all the answers. At times just a hug, a smile, listening, or just being there is the best counsel.

Some pastors will work with a person for years. Others, perhaps for the sake of the church, or for the well being of themselves, or the client, they will separate from a person who does not cease from sin (I Cor. 5:11). It may be wisdom not to expect or push for change for a year or two but it can be very frustrating to wait ten years for people to "get with it." It is well known that alcoholics may not stop drinking until they hit bottom. Dying to self can be a difficult life-long process (Lk. 17:33, Ro. 6:11, Gal. 2:20 & 5:24, Col. 3:2).

For most of us it is a good idea to have therapeutic leverage applied in the manner of a judo expert rather than being embroiled in a head to head boxing match. Tough love means to require responsibility and accountability. It does not mean yelling or fighting with a client. As much as is possible each individual's integrity, dignity, potential, and freedom should be honored.

What is proper or considered acceptable in each case may differ to some degree. The client needs to have hope, to at least be willing to try and to be willing to take responsible action. Not all arrive this way (Pro. 13:12). Counseling has been called a battle of wills; a process of working through resistance to change or denial.

Several requests have been made for a follow-up "how to" book with answers. I recently took another course in family therapy. The tuition was $350, the 400 page textbook cost $50 (used), the other recommended reading cost $35 (used), and the workbook was $20. This was for a two hour, two nights a week, eight week course. Some of the ideas I learned there have been put into this book. However, I do not claim to be expert in them. there is no quick and easy cookbook for counseling. There are over 100 techniques given in this book, as well as over 100 books listed in the Bibliography. Learning to use them takes time and training, and there is no guarantee they will help.

My hope is that this book will give an overview that will help ministers in their work. It will have succeeded if anyone finds a clue or comfort from it. People either like its breadth, clarity, and honesty, or fault its lack of depth, or object to combining a spiritual and natural view, or call a frank discussion of problems "negativity." Many of the issues raised in this book on: the use of labels, degrees of severity, and finding a balance between truth, love, grace, and mercy, remain to be dealt with by each reader. I welcome comment.

One of the latest books out on Biblical counseling is by a scholar who simply rejects all supernatural gifts. This intellectual dishonesty is in accord with the position of his denomination. The result is a mechanical, almost legalistic, use of scripture. He manages to lean heavily on psychology without acknowledging it. Another very popular book on marriage relationships is by a secular psychologist who has no other credentials (he is not an Rev.).but somehow the work is called "Christian." Another secular book on counseling, that has been hugely successful, seems to have resulted in many more people being sold on trying psycho-therapy. There are, of course, many books available that do not create or support a myth, a lie, or denial.

One pastor remarked that nothing in this book related to the counseling he did. He then explained his work by using personality types from discredited Greek philosophy. Another pastor thought myths did not affect him. However, he complained about what his children were taught in public school.

Some pastors have said they appreciated this book for all that it had in it. They especially liked it because it included a Full(er) Gospel that is not simply one testimony after another of miracles that do not seem to happen to the people they know. For many however, *psychology* is still taboo. The news media can be counted on to broadcast the most bizarre cases, but they often leave out the full story. Most of the above responses came from friends of mine.

An Enemy of the People (1882), by Henrik Ibsen, tells the story of a doctor whose house was stoned and burned down by his patients. These people worked in a factory that was making them sick. The doctor's reports on pollution threatened the village's economy. Instead of correcting the problem the messenger was stoned and driven away, It still happens today.

However it manifests, **sin is deceitful**; in science, religion, or in our own personal lives (Heb. 3:13). There are those who adamantly reject any attacks on "science," even bad science, out of a fear of being associated with the "fanatical religious right." The "fanatical secular left" does most of the hiring and firing. It may be that the theology and doctrines of this book are not acceptable to some groups. That means there may be fewer books sold.

Any time we attempt to manipulate factors in a person's life to cause change, even a slight suggestion, with reinforcement or sanctions, we could be called "behaviorists." When we speak about life and death, or a sense of self and responsibility, we can be called "existentialists." Sharing a painful past, or listening to another person's testimony of grief, can be labeled “psycho-dynamic” counseling. Affirming the resurrection of Jesus from the dead, sharing a scripture, or praying with someone, is all it takes to be called a "Christian counselor." We often do these things without any advanced education or special credentials. We are all human. We have certain similar experiences, abilities, and needs.

Placing scriptures in the context of modern counseling demonstrates the preeminence of the Holy Bible. The secular counseling theories give some useful structure and organization. Although ancient Biblical wisdom and modern psychology may seem similar in certain ways, they are not identical.

Whether renamed or amplified, the Scripture still has eternal value. Counseling is often referred to as an art. Creativity is required for us to develop effective counseling techniques to apply Biblical truths. Love is needed to sustain them. The goal is spiritual wholeness in the fulfillment of God's purposes. There-in is true joy (Ps. 16:11).

Our creative nature, and the power of love have their place. However, science and technique only rarely move the heart of man. Art can help explain and inspire; sculpture, painting, music, dance, literature or poetry can move us. A meeting with God, who is Love, and fellowship with our Creator, can move and change us so much more.

The spiritual, the mind of God, not the mind of man, is the most important point to consider. God instituted worship and He hates idolatry. He built a beautiful temple with a garden, and put an image in it, where He went to worship. He communed and fellowshipped with the idol (image of God) that He had made and it reflected His image. Then, in order to more clearly reflect His glory He gave us free choice.

We used this gift to create our own idols of ourselves; images of how we can function best, separate from God. Rather than simply being a reflection of our Creator we create and worship reflections of ourselves. **We were created in the image of God, to fellowship with Him, and to reflect His Glory**. (Gen. 1:26, II Cor. 3:18).

The patchwork quilt of church activities includes preaching and teaching, and also being part of smaller care and share groups for nurturing and instruction. Opportunities for giving and for service abound. There is time for teamwork, and for one-on-one relationships with peers and with more mature Christians. Leadership and travel experiences may occur. The tapestry of a Christian's life is made up of times of corporate worship, private Bible study and prayer, and personal devotional time with the Lord. The Holy rituals of: dedication, baptism, confirmation, communion, anointing of the sick, anointing for offices, as well as marriages, and funerals, all help give order to our lives, while we are being clothed upon with His righteous gown.

A pastor who is swamped with counseling, rather than being occupied with building these church activities, is missing the ark. These are the things that create and contribute to mental and spiritual health. Bringing a person to where he or she can participate in church may be the sole goal of counseling, other than during times of crisis.

We are approaching the times of restitution of all things when the light of the Truth shall expose all darkness and the Truth shall be revealed (Acts 3:21). As we get nearer, more is revealed to those who are open to receive it. The "...race is not to the swift, nor the battle to the strong..." (Ecc. 9:11).

Dr. Carl Henry noted that much of what passes for Christianity today is nothing more than an apostate compromise with the spirit of the age. Both Greek philosophy and science falsely so-called are part of that mixture. "What can we use, and what results can we expect?" Many pastors in their mid 30's feel their job requires 40 years of experience and wisdom. "What can we realistically expect to accomplish?" I trust this book has helped examine these issues.

William Tuke, a Quaker who founded the York Retreat in England during the 18th century, rejected the cruel and barbaric psychiatry and medical "expertise" of his day. He felt exposure to a normal, God-fearing, household was all that was needed to restore even the most troubled individual of his time. That asylum is still in operation today, for those who can afford it.

Spurgeon once wrote: "the nerve of prayer is that thin thread which moves the muscle of omnipotence." In our world today we have to deal with people with Fetal Alcohol Syndrome, and children born addicted to crack cocaine. This would be unbearable without the power of prayer.

Prayer, repentance, and revival are the ultimate answers. These should not be used to deny or ignore the problems we have to deal with now, before we reach the ultimate. The Evangelical belief in the supernatural and the inerrancy of scripture, is not the same as a presumptuous use of the Bible made in the name of "faith" (Deut. 18:20-22, Ps. 19:13).

To be "more than a conqueror" (Ro. 8:31 & 37), means to be a giver of life. **Ministries are given for the "perfecting" or equipping of the saints** (Eph. 4:11-12). In the Greek this has the sense of: **repairing, mending, or restoring** (#2675 in Strong's Concordance). **With God's help we can.** (Ps. 147:3, Is. 35:4, 40:1, & 11, 41:6, 53:4 & 5, Joel 2:25, Lk. 19:10, Jn. 3:16-17, Acts 20:35, Gal. 6:9, I Thes. 5:14, Jude 22, I Jn. 2:25). **He told us to try,** to occupy profitably until He comes (Lk. 19:13).

Counseling by family members and friends is the usual means of maintaining mental health. However, there are many problems and situations that can only be understood by someone who has experienced them (II Cor. 1:3-4). Helping others is feasible if the experiences have been handled well, or if a person has had some training. It is possible to be more than just a kind-hearted but floundering rescuer. Like Helen Keller's teacher, Annie Sullivan, counselors and pastors may be justifiably called miracle workers.

Chapter XII Review

Have you had to counsel someone facing transplant surgery? What about the issue of buying and selling, or growing, body parts for transplant? What do you tell someone who is in such great pain that he or she is considering euthanasia? What is the latest medical definition of "dead?" Do you want to pay for enormously expensive care and high tech medicine for someone who will never get better? It seems wasteful to some, others want it.

There are many more issues to explore that have not been included in this book. *"Bio-ethics*;" the newest face of the "fear of death," and the "pride of life," is just one. We can explore them honestly and acknowledge our real desires. Our fear and pride can be dealt with. Myths, lies, and denial will however, continue to be major challenges counselors and pastors face.

(Scripture references for chapter XII)

pg. 209

Ecc. 12:13 - Let us hear the conclusion of the whole matter: Fear God, and keep his commandments: for this [is] the whole [duty] of man.

Ex. 18:23 - if thou shalt do this thing, and God commands thee so, then thou shalt be able to endure, and all this people shall also go to their place in peace.

Num. 11:17 - ...and they shall bear the burden of the people with thee, that thou bear it not thyself alone.

pg. 211
I Cor. 5:11 - ...I have written unto you not to keep company, if any man that is called a brother be a fornicator
or covetous, or an idolater, or a railer, or a drunkard, or an extortioner; with such an one no not to eat.

Luke 17:33 - Whosoever shall seek to save his life shall lose it; and whosoever shall lose his life shall preserve it.

Ro. 6:11 - ...reckon ye also yourselves to be dead indeed unto sin, but alive unto God through Jesus Christ our Lord.

Gal. 2:20 & 5:24 - I am crucified with Christ: nevertheless I live; yet not I, but Christ liveth in me: and the life which I now live in the flesh I live by the faith of the Son of God, who loved me, and gave himself for me. **(24)** And they that are Christ's have crucified the flesh with the affections and lusts.

Col. 3:2 - Set your affections on things above, not on things on the earth.

pg. 212
Pro. 13:12 - Hope deferred maketh the heart sick: but [when] the desire cometh, [it is] a tree of life.

pg. 214
Heb. 3:13 - ...lest any of you be hardened through the deceitfulness of sin.

pg.215
Ps. 16:11 - thou will shew me the path of life: in thy
presence is fullness of joy...

pg. 216
Gen. 1:26 - And God said, Let us make man in our image, after our likeness: and let them have dominion...

II Cor. 3:18 - But we all, with open face beholding as in a glass the glory of the Lord, are changed into the same image from glory to glory, [even] as by the Spirit of the Lord.

pg. 217 - Acts 3:21...until the times of restitution of all things...

Ecc. 9:11. ...the race is not to the swift, nor the battle to the strong...

pg. 218 - Deut. 18:20-22 - But the prophet, which shall presume to speak a word in my name, which I have not commanded him to speak, or that shall speak in the name of other gods, even that prophet shall die. **(21)** And if thou say in thine heart, How shall we know the word which the LORD hath not spoken? **(22)** When a prophet speaketh in the name of the LORD, if the thing follow not, nor come to pass, that [is] the thing which the LORD hath not spoken, [but] the prophet hath spoken it presumptuously: thou shalt not be afraid of him.

Ps. 19:13 - Keep back thy servant also from presumptuous [sins].

Ro. 8:31 & 37 - ...if God [be] for us, who [can be] against us? (37) Nay, in all these things we are more than conquerors through him that loved us.

Eph. 4:11-12 - And he gave some, apostles... prophets... evangelists... pastors and teachers; **(12)** For the perfecting of the saints... for the edifying of the body of Christ:

Ps. 147:3 - He healeth the broken in heart, and bindeth up their wounds.

Is. 35:4 - Say to them [that are] of a fearful heart, Be strong, fear not: behold, your God will come... [with] a recompence; he will come and save you.

Is. 40:1 & 11 - Comfort ye, comfort ye my people, saith your God. **(11)** - He shall feed his flock like a shepherd: he shall gather the lambs with his arm, and carry [them] in his bosom, [and] shall gently lead those that are with young.

Is. 41:6 & 53:4-5 - They helped every one his neighbour; and [every one] said to his brother, Be of good courage. **(4)** Surely he hath borne our griefs, and carried our sorrows: yet we did esteem him stricken, smitten of God, and afflicted. **(5)** But he [was] wounded for our transgressions, [he was] bruised for our iniquities: the chastisement of our peace [was] upon him; and with his stripes we are healed.

Joel 2:25 - **(25)** And I will restore to you the years that the locust hath eaten,

Luke 19:10 - For the Son of Man is come to seek and to save that which was lost.

John 3:16-17 - For God so loved the world, that he gave his only begotten Son, that whosoever believeth in him should not perish, but have everlasting life. **(17)** For God sent not his Son into the world to condemn the world; but that the world through him might be saved.

Acts 20:35 - ...ye ought to support the weak...

Gal. 6:9 - And let us not be weary in well doing: for in due season we shall reap, if we faint not.

I Thes. 5:14 - ... comfort the feebleminded, support the weak, be patient toward all [men].

I Jn. 2:25 - ...he hath promised us, [even] eternal life.

Jude 22 - ...have compassion, making a difference:...

Lk. 19:13 - And he called his... servants,... and said unto them, Occupy till I come.

II Cor. 1:3-4 - Blessed [be] God, even the Father of Our Lord Jesus Christ, the Father of mercies, and the God of all comfort; (4) Who comforteth us in all our tribulation, that we may be able to comfort them which are in any trouble, by the comfort wherewith we ourselves are comforted of God.

Bibliography

Adams, Jay, (1986 rev.). Competent To Counsel. Grand Rapids, MI.: Zondervan.

Allander, D., (1990). The Wounded Heart: Hope for the adult victim of childhood sexual abuse. Colorado Springs, CO.: NavPress.

American Psychiatric Association, (1994). The Diagnostic And Statistical Manual Of Mental Disorders (4th ed.) (5 ed. 2013). Washington, D.C.: American Psychiatric Association.

Arterburn, Stephen, & Felton, Jack, (1991). Toxic Faith: Overcoming religious addiction. Nashville, TN.:Thomas Nelson.

B, Mel, (1991). New Wine: The spiritual roots of the 12 step miracle. Center City, MN.: Hazelden.

Babgan, Michael & Deidre, (1987). Psycho-Heresy: The psychological seduction of Christianity. Santa Barbara, CA.: Eastgate.

Bass, Ellen & Davis, Laura (1988). The Courage To Heal. N.Y., NY.: Harper Perennial. (childhood sexual abuse)

Benner, David, G., (1990). Healing Emotional Wounds. Grand Rapids, MI.: Baker Book House.

Bennett, Dennis & Rita, (1971). The Holy Spirit and You. Plainfield, NJ.: Logos, International.

Berkow, R. (ed.) (16th edition), (1992) (19th edition. 2011). The Merck Manual of Diagnosis and Therapy. Rahway, NJ.:Merck Research Lab. (medical diagnosis and treatment)

Bole, T. J. III, (1990). The ordinary/extraordinary distinction: A moral context for the proper calculus of benefits and burdens. Hospital Ethics Committee (HEC) Forum. 2 (June 4), pp. 217-227. (Bio-Ethics)

Brenner, R. R., (1980). Faith and Doubt Of Holocaust Survivors. N.Y., NY.: The Free Press.

Bresson, B. L., (1966). Studies In Ecstasy. N.Y., NY.: Vantage Press. (A history of manifestations of the Holy Spirit)

Brodwin, M., Telles, F., Brodwin, S., (1992). Medical, Psycho-social, and Vocational Aspects of Disability. Athens, GA.: Elliot & Fitzpatrick Inc.

Bromely, C.W., (ed.) (1979). The International Standard Bible Encyclopedia. (4 vols.) Grand Rapids, MI.: Eerdman's.

Buskey, J. R., (1994). Binding Up The Brokenhearted. Contact Dr. Buskey at 3350 N. Key Drive, N. Fort Myers, FL. 33903, or write to Pinecrest Publications, Salisbury Center, NY. 13454 (A manual on Inner Healing)

CBN, (1987). The Christian Counselor's Handbook. Wheaton, IL.: Tyndale House.

Cairns, E., (1967). Christianity Through The Ages. Grand Rapids, MI.: Zondervan.

Caram, Paul, (1990). Victory Over The Self-Centered Life. Christian Maturity Series. Box 256, Ulysses, PA.16948.: Zion Christian Assembly.

Coles, R., (1990). The Spiritual Life Of Children. Boston, MA.: Houghton Mifflin.

Collins, Gary, (1988 revised). Christian Counseling: A comprehensive guide. Irvine, TX.: Word.

Collins, Gary, (1993). The Biblical Basis of Christian Counseling for People Helpers. Colorado Springs, CO.: NavPress.

Collins, Gary, (ed.) (1995). Resources for Christian Counselors, Series. (30+ vols.) Dallas, TX.: Word.

Corsini, Raymond, & Wedding, Danny, (1991). Current Psychotherapies. 4th ed. Itasca, IL.: F.E. Peacock.

Corsini, Raymond, & Wedding, Danny, (1989). Case Studies In Psychotherapy. Itasca, IL.: F.E. Peacock.

Crabb, Larry, (1988). Inside Out. Colorado Springs, CO.: NavPress.

Davis, Laura, (1991). Allies In Healing. N.Y., NY.: Harper Perennial. (childhood sexual abuse)

Dobson, J., (1983). Love Must Be Tough. (1987) Parenting Isn't For Cowards Dallas, TX.: Word. (1993). When God Doesn't Make Sense. Wheaton, IL.: Tyndale House.

Doka, Kenneth, J., (ed.), (1995). Children Mourning - Mourning Children. Washington D.C.: The Hospice Foundation of America.

Elkin, Michael, (1984). Families Under The Influence: changing alcoholic patterns. N.Y.: W.W. Norton & Co.

Ells, A., (1990). Restoring Innocence. Nashville, TN. Thomas Nelson. (childhood sexual abuse)

Engler, Jack & Goleman, Daniel, (1992). The Consumers Guide To Therapy. N.Y., NY.: Simon & Schuster.

Enroth, R., (1992). Churches That Abuse. Grand Rapids, MI.: Zondervan.

Farr, J. M., (1991). The Very Quick Job Search. Indianapolis, IN.: JEST Works Inc.

Filmakers Library, Questions of Life and Death, a video collection covering multiple topics: dearth and dying, living with illness, AIDS, addictions.124 East 40th st. N.Y., NY.

Finney, C., (1978). Revivals of Religion. Va. Bch, VA.: CBN University Press.

Foley, B., (1992). Handbook On Restorative Therapy: A Psycho-Spiritual Developmental Model. 217 Babbit Hill Rd., Pomfret Center, CT.

Forward, Susan (1989). Toxic Parents. N.Y., NY.: Bantam Books. (physical, sexual , and, verbal childhood abuse.)

Frankl, V., (1963). Man's Search For Meaning: an introduction to Logotherapy. N.Y.: Pocket Books.

Freeman, D., (1983). Margaret Mead and Samoa: The making and unmaking of an anthropological myth. Boston, MA.: Harvard Univ. Press.

Ganong, L. & Coleman, M., (1989). Preparing for remarriage: Anticipating the issues, seeking solutions. Journal of Applied Family and Child Studies. 38(1), pp. 8-33.

Ganz, R., (1993). Psycho Babble: The failure of modern psychology and the Biblical alternative. Wheaton, IL.: Crossway Books.

Goldenberg, I. & H., (1991). Family Therapy: An Overview. 3rd. ed. Belmont, CA.: Brooks/Cole, Wadsworth Inc.

Hamner, T. & Turner, P., (1985). Parenting In Contemporary Society. Englewood Cliffs, NJ.: Prentice Hall.

Harrell Jr., D. (1975). All Things Are Possible: The Healing and Charismatic Revivals In Modern America. Bloomington and London: Indiana University Press.

Hart, A., (1988). How To Handle Anger and Resentment. Irving, TX.: Word.

Heifetz, L., (1987). Integrating religious and secular perspectives in the design and delivery of disability services. Mental Retardation. 25 (3), pp. 127-131.

Hendrix, H., (1990). Getting The Love You Want. N.Y., NY.: Harper Colliers.

Henry, Carl, (ed.) (1971). Basic Christian Doctrines Grand Rapids, MI.: Baker Book House.

Holmes, Arthur, (1977). All Truth Is God's Truth. Downers Grove, IL.: Intervarsity Press.

Hunt, David, (1985). The Seduction Of Christianity, Eugene, OR.: Harvest House.

Huse, S., (1992). The Collapse of Evolution. Grand Rapids, MI.: Baker Book House.

Johnson, P., (1991). Darwin On Trial. Downers Grove, IL: Intervarsity Press.

Kaplan, H.J. & Sadock, B.J., (1989). The Comprehensive Textbook of Psychiatry (5th ed.). Baltimore, MD.: William & Wilkens.

Kennedy, J., (1965). The Torch Of The Testimony. Auburn, ME.: Christian Books Publishing House.

Kierkagaard, S., (1956). Purity of Heart Is To Will One Thing. N.Y., NY.: Harper & Row.

Kirk, S., & Kutchins, H., (1992). The Selling of DSM: The rhetoric of science in psychiatry. Hawthorne, NY. Aldine de Gruyter.

Kubler-Ross, E., (1974). Questions & Answers On Death and Dying. N.Y., NY: Collier Books.

LaHaye, T. & B., (1976). The Act of Marriage. Grand Rapids, MI.: Zondervan.

Lake, F., (1987). Clinical Theology, A Theological and Psychiatric Basis to Clinical Pastoral Care. N.Y.,NY. Crossroads.

Lawson, G.W., Ellis, D.C., & Rivers, C.P., (1984). Essentials of Chemical Dependency Counseling. Maryland: Aspen.

Levicoff, S., (1991). Christian Counseling And The Law. Chicago, IL.: Moody Press.

Lewis, C.S., (1943). Christian Behavior. (1962). The Problem Of Pain. N.Y., NY.: MacMillan & Co.

Liberman, R.P., Wheeler, E., deVisser, L.A., Kuehnel J., & Kuehnel, T. (1980). Handbook of Marital Therapy, New York: Plenum.

Liberty, Leona, (1990). Counselor: National certification and state licensing preparation CRC & NCC. N.Y.: ARCO, Prentice Hall.

Masson, Jeffery M., (1984). The Assault On Truth: Freud's suppression of the seduction theory. N.Y., NY.: Ferrac, Straus, & Giroux. (Contains graphic, vile material.)

McDowell, Josh, (1993). Evidence That Demands A Verdict. (Vol I). (1993). Evidence That Demands A Verdict (Vol II), Nashville, TN.: Thomas Nelson.

Menninger, Karl, (1973). Whatever Became of Sin? N.Y., NY.: Hawthorn Books.

Merinelli, R.P., & Dell Orto, A.E., (1991). The Psychological and Social Aspects of Disability. N.Y., NY.: Springer.

Millard, C., (1991). The Re-writing Of American History. Camphill, PA.: Horizon House.

Miller, J. E. (1994), How Can I help? What Can Help Me? Fort Wayne, IN.: Willow Green.

Milton, L. R., (1979). Christian Ethics For Today: An Evangelical Approach. Grand Rapids, MI.: Baker Book House.

Minirth, P. & Byrd, W., (1990). Christian Psychiatry. Old Tappan, NJ.: Revell.

Minirth, F. & Meier, P., (1990). Love Hunger: Co-dependent relationships. Nashville, TN.: Thomas Nelson.

Minuchin, S., (1993). Family Healing: Tales of hope and renewal from family therapy. New York, NY.: Free Press.

Montigue, G. T., (1974) The Spirit and His Gifts. N.Y., NY.: Paulist Press.

Murphy, E., (1992). Handbook For Spiritual Warfare. Nashville, TN.: Thomas Nelson.

Murray, J., (1974). Principles of Conduct: Aspects of Biblical Ethics. Grand Rapids, MI.: Wm. B. Eerdman.

Nee, Watchman, (1980). The Normal Christian Life Wheaton, IL.: Tyndale.

Oates, W., (1982). Pastoral Counseling. (1987). Behind The Masks: Personality Disorders in Religious Behavior. Louisville, KY.: Westminster, John Knox.

Peale, N. V., (1952). The Power of Positive Thinking N.Y., NY.: Prentice Hall. and (1981). Dynamic Imaging. N.Y., NY.: Revell.

Price, C., (1972). The Real Faith. Plainfield, NJ.: Logos.

Reisman, Judith A. & Eichel, Edward W., (1990). Kinsey: Sex and Fraud: the indoctrination of a people. Lafayette, LA.: Huntington House, Lochinvar Inc.

Sandford, J. & P., (1982). The Transformation Of The Inner Man. (1985) Healing The Wounded Spirit. (1987) Restoring The Christian Family. Tulsa, OK.: Victory House.

Satir, V., (1982). Conjoint Family Therapy (3rd ed.). (1987). The New Peoplemaking. Palo Alto, CA.:Science and Behavior Books.

Satir, V., Bannan, J., Gerber, J., & Gomari, M. (1991). The Satir Model: Family Therapy and Beyond. Palo Alto, CA.: Science and Behavior Books.

Sears, W., (1991). Christian Parenting and Child Care. Nashville, TN.: Thomas Nelson.

Shaeffer, Francis, (1976), How Should We Then Live. Westchester, IL.: Crossway Books.

Smalley, G. & Trent, J., (1986). The Blessing. N.Y., NY.: Pocket Books.

Solomon, David, (1992). A Consumers Guide To Aging. Baltimore, MD.: John Hopkins Univ. Press.

Spitzer, R., (et al.) (1994). Casebook: Diagnostic and Statistical Manual of Mental Disorders (DSM-IV).Wash. D.C.: Amer. Psychiatric Assoc. Press.

Stuart, R.B. (1980). Helping Couples Change, Champaign, IL.: Research Press.

Taylor, Wade, (1993). The Secret of the Stairs. (1996). Waterspouts of Glory. (2012) Being Made Ready, A daily devotional. Wade Taylor Publications, 1-800-349-0340. www.wadetaylorpublications.org

Thomas à Kempis, (1910). The Imitation of Christ. N.Y.: E.P. Dutton & Co.

Thomas, C., (ed.) (1993) (17th Edition), Taber's Cyclopedic Medical Dictionary. Philadelphia, PA.: F.A. Davis Co. (2017). (23rd Edition, Online Edition).

Tillich, P., (1952). The Courage To Be. New Haven, CT.: Yale University Press.

Tournier, P., (1965). The Healing of Persons. N.Y., N.Y.: Harper & Row.

Tozer, A.W., (1948). The Pursuit of God. Harrison, PA.: Christian Publications. (2016) The Purpose of Man Bethany House, Baker, Grand Rapids, MI.

Train, R., (1980). Methodical Bible Study. Wilmore, KY.: Asbury Theological Seminary.

Williams, J. R., (1980). The Gift of the Holy Spirit Today. Plainfield, NJ.: Logos International.

Wright, N., (1977). Training Christians To Counsel. Eugene, OR.: Harvest House.

Scriptures of the Holy Bible are from the Authorized King James Version (1611) unless otherwise noted.

For further study into the myths mentioned in Myths, Lies, and Denial, the following books are recommended:

Babgan, Michael & Deidre, (1987). Psycho-Heresy: The psychological seduction of Christianity. Santa Barbara, CA.: Eastgate.

Freeman, D., (1983). Margaret Mead and Samoa: The making and unmaking of an anthropological myth., Boston, MA.: Harvard Univ. Press.

Ganz, R., (1993). Psycho Babble: The failure of modern psychology and the Biblical alternative. Wheaton, IL.: Crossway Books.

Huse, S., (1992). The Collapse of Evolution. Grand Rapids, MI.: Baker Book House.

Johnson, P., (1991). Darwin On Trial. Downers Grove, IL.: Intervarsity Press.

Kirk, S., & Kutchins, H., (1992). The Selling of DSM: The rhetoric of science in psychiatry. Hawthorne, NY.: Aldine de Gruyter.

Masson, Jeffery M., (1984). The Assault On Truth: Freud's suppression of the seduction theory. N.Y.NY.: Ferrac, Strauss, & Giroux. (This is a medical book and is very graphic, perhaps too vile for most readers.)

McDowell, Josh, (1993). Evidence That Demands A Verdict. (vols. I & II). Nashville, TN.: Thomas Nelson.

Millard, C., (1991). The Re-writing Of American History Camphill, PA.: Horizon House.

Reisman, Judith A. & Eichel, Edward W., (1990). Kinsey: Sex and Fraud: the indoctrination of a people. Lafayette, LA.: Huntington House, Lochinvar Inc.

About the author

Dr. John Jay Frank, for years an Ordained Minister of the Gospel (Rev.) and a Licensed Professional Counselor (LPC, OH) and a Certified Rehabilitation Counselor (CRC), has had training in Biblical Studies and counseling. His doctorate (Ph.D. 2003) Is from the Counselor and Human Services Department at Syracuse University. He received a Certificate of Endorsement, Alliance Chaplain, from the Christian and Missionary Alliance and was a member of the American Association of Christian Counselors (AACC).

Dr. Frank is the founder of Minstrel Missions LLC. He writes articles and books, and records songs and hymns for the education, edification, encouragement, and comfort of the body of Christ. See: www.minstrelmissions.com, or e-mail questions to: minstrelmissions@gmail.com

3 Books:

Turning Barriers Into Bridges: The Inclusive Use of Information and Communication Technology for Churches in America, Britain, and Canada

Myths, Lies, & Denial: Christian and Secular Counseling in America

A Minstrel's Notes: Stories and Sermons on Worship in Spirit and In Truth, and Music Theory and Technique for the Acoustic Guitar

6 Music Recordings (CDs):

For All God's Children
Comfort Ye My People
The Cross Of Life
Hymns of the Church
Hymns and Carols
Hymns of God's Grace

A music DVD: Pick'n and Preach'n (films of songs performed in Connecticut and California.)

www.ingramcontent.com/pod-product-compliance
Lightning Source LLC
LaVergne TN
LVHW020042110826
845155LV00029B/609

* 9 7 8 1 8 8 7 8 3 5 0 0 8 *